S0-AWE-532

Domestic Extremism

Other Books in the Current Controversies Series

Domestic Extremism

Eamon Doyle, Book Editor

GREENHAVEN
PUBLISHING

Published in 2022 by Greenhaven Publishing, LLC
353 3rd Avenue, Suite 255, New York, NY 10010

Copyright © 2022 by Greenhaven Publishing, LLC

First Edition

All rights reserved. No part of this book may be reproduced in any form
without permission in writing from the publisher, except by a reviewer.

Articles in Greenhaven Publishing anthologies are often edited for length to meet page
requirements. In addition, original titles of these works are changed to clearly present
the main thesis and to explicitly indicate the author's opinion. Every effort is made to
ensure that Greenhaven Publishing accurately reflects the original intent of the authors.
Every effort has been made to trace the owners of the copyrighted material.

Cover image: Johnny Silvercloud/Shutterstock.com

Library of Congress Cataloging-in-Publication Data

Names: Doyle, Eamon, 1988- editor.
Title: Domestic extremism / Eamon Doyle, book editor.
Description: First edition. | New York : Greenhaven Publishing, 2022. |
    Series: Current controversies | Includes bibliographical references and
    index. | Audience: Ages 15+ | Audience: Grades 10-12 | Summary:
    "Anthology of diverse viewpoints exploring extremists on both the right
    and the left, how domestic extremism has evolved since the advent of the
    internet and social media, and how law enforcement at various levels
    should address it, particularly in the prevention of extremist
    attacks"-- Provided by publisher.
Identifiers: LCCN 2021031626 | ISBN 9781534508507 (library binding) | ISBN
    9781534508491 (paperback) | ISBN 9781534508514 (ebook)
Subjects: LCSH: Radicalism--United States--Juvenile literature. | Right and
    left (Political science)--United States--Juvenile literature.
Classification: LCC HN90.R3 D66 2022 | DDC 303.48/40973--dc23
LC record available at https://lccn.loc.gov/2021031626

Manufactured in the United States of America

Website: http://greenhavenpublishing.com

Contents

Chapter 1: Do Political Parties Encourage Extremism in the US?

Didi Kuo

This viewpoint examines the structural role of parties in governing a state as well as the rhetorical, cultural, and political dynamics that often emerge in a party-centric system. While political parties are not inherently problematic for democracy, there are a number of potential problems and challenges that they raise.

Yes: Political Parties Encourage Citizens to View Democratic Politics Through an "Us vs. Them" Framework

Alexis Blue

Negative partisanship in the social media environment has encouraged more political participation and higher voter turnout, but is the type of participation associated with negative partisanship healthy for democracy?

Pew Research Center

American attitudes about the social safety net, race, and immigration appear to be diverging along mostly partisan lines. Perhaps most concerning, these and other such partisan divisions are becoming even more pronounced and consequential than divisions based on race, gender, or ethnicity.

No: Political Parties Almost Always Play an Essential Role in the Structure and Organization of Stable Democratic Societies

Russell Muirhead and Nancy L. Rosenblum

This viewpoint explores the concepts of dynamic and institutional pluralism and argues that parties play a central role in democratizing representative government. There is no guarantee that representative government will remain democratic in the absence of parties.

Chapter 2: Is Political Extremism a Significant Cause of Terrorism and Violent Crime in the US?

election was tainted by voter fraud. This alignment has increased the risk of violence associated with the far right.

Jaclyn Diaz and Rachel Treisman

Many of the participants of the January 6 riot at the US Capitol were prepared not only to engage in violence but to execute public officials (including, notably, former vice president Mike Pence) who resisted their demands.

Lois Beckett and Josh Horwitz

The concept of violent, anti-government insurrection is something of a core value among Second Amendment extremists. Politicians and law enforcement officials should take the threats associated with gun and militia culture seriously and prepare for the likelihood that at least some will eventually engage in acts of political violence.

Alexander Hinton

In this viewpoint, the author identifies five separate reasons why the American intelligence and law enforcement community should treat the threat of violence from right-wing groups seriously.

No: Political Polarization in Contemporary American Society Is Unlikely to Result in Significant Instances of Violence

Chip Gibbons

Americans should be wary of law enforcement strategies designed to target political extremism. The FBI's use of "radicalization theory" has opened the door to more political surveillance and a slippery slope with regard to First Amendment rights.

David Smith

Conservatives highlight socialism as the central threat to contemporary American democracy. Their narrative of Democrats as a party full of dangerous communists is a new Red Scare that could distract from dangerous right-wing activity.

Chapter 3: Does the Contemporary Media Environment in America Encourage Political Extremism?

Yes: Multiple Conditions in the Contemporary Media Environment Are Contributing to Political Extremism in America

No: The Media Environment Is an Attractive Target for Critics Who Are Worried About Political Extremism's Effect on Democracy

the arbitrary decisions of unaccountable corporations to determine what is allowed and disallowed.

Foreword

"Controversy" is a word that has an undeniably unpleasant connotation. It carries a definite negative charge. Controversy can spoil family gatherings, spread a chill around classroom and campus discussion, inflame public discourse, open raw civic wounds, and lead to the ouster of public officials. We often feel that controversy is almost akin to bad manners, a rude and shocking eruption of that which must not be spoken or thought of in polite, tightly guarded society. To avoid controversy, to quell controversy, is often seen as a public good, a victory for etiquette, perhaps even a moral or ethical imperative.

Yet the studious, deliberate avoidance of controversy is also a whitewashing, a denial, a death threat to democracy. It is a false sterilizing and sanitizing and superficial ordering of the messy, ragged, chaotic, at times ugly processes by which a healthy democracy identifies and confronts challenges, engages in passionate debate about appropriate approaches and solutions, and arrives at something like a consensus and a broadly accepted and supported way forward. Controversy is the megaphone, the speaker's corner, the public square through which the citizenry finds and uses its voice. Controversy is the life's blood of our democracy and absolutely essential to the vibrant health of our society.

Our present age is certainly no stranger to controversy. We are consumed by fierce debates about technology, privacy, political correctness, poverty, violence, crime and policing, guns, immigration, civil and human rights, terrorism, militarism, environmental protection, and gender and racial equality. Loudly competing voices are raised every day, shouting opposing opinions, putting forth competing agendas, and summoning starkly different visions of a utopian or dystopian future. Often these voices attempt to shout the others down; there is precious little listening and considering among the cacophonous din. Yet listening and considering, too, are essential to the health of a democracy. If controversy is democracy's lusty lifeblood, respectful listening and careful thought are its higher faculties, its brain, its conscience.

Current Controversies does not shy away from or attempt to hush the loudly competing voices. It seeks to provide readers with as wide and representative as possible a range of articulate voices on any given controversy of the day, separates each one out to allow it to be heard clearly and fairly, and encourages careful listening to each of these well-crafted, thoughtfully expressed opinions, supplied by some of today's leading academics, thinkers, analysts, politicians, policy makers, economists, activists, change agents, and advocates. Only after listening to a wide range of opinions on an issue, evaluating the strengths and weaknesses of each argument, assessing how well the facts and available evidence mesh with the stated opinions and conclusions, and thoughtfully and critically examining one's own beliefs and conscience can the reader begin to arrive at his or her own conclusions and articulate his or her own stance on the spotlighted controversy.

This process is facilitated and supported in each Current Controversies volume by an introduction and chapter overviews that provide readers with the essential context they need to begin engaging with the spotlighted controversies, with the debates surrounding them, and with their own perhaps shifting or nascent opinions on them. Chapters are organized around several key questions that are answered with diverse opinions representing all points on the political spectrum. In its content, organization, and methodology, readers are encouraged to determine the authors' point of view and purpose, interrogate and analyze the various arguments and their rhetoric and structure, evaluate the arguments' strengths and weaknesses, test their claims against available facts and evidence, judge the validity of the reasoning, and bring into clearer, sharper focus the reader's own beliefs and conclusions and how they may differ from or align with those in the collection or those of classmates.

Research has shown that reading comprehension skills improve dramatically when students are provided with compelling, intriguing, and relevant "discussable" texts. The subject matter of these collections could not be more compelling, intriguing, or urgently relevant to today's students and the world they are poised to inherit. The anthologized articles also provide the basis for stimulating, lively, and passionate classroom debates. Students who are compelled to anticipate objections to their own argument and identify the flaws in those of an opponent read more carefully, think more critically, and steep themselves in relevant context, facts, and information more thoroughly. In short, using discussable text of the kind provided by every single volume in the Current Controversies series encourages close reading, facilitates reading comprehension, fosters research, strengthens critical thinking, and greatly enlivens and energizes classroom discussion and participation. The entire learning process is deepened, extended, and strengthened.

If we are to foster a knowledgeable, responsible, active, and engaged citizenry, we must provide readers with the intellectual, interpretive, and critical-thinking tools and experience necessary to make sense of the world around them and of the all-important debates and arguments that inform it. We must encourage them not to run away from or attempt to quell controversy but to embrace it in a responsible, conscientious, and thoughtful way, to sharpen and strengthen their own informed opinions by listening to and critically analyzing those of others. This series encourages respectful engagement with and analysis of current controversies and competing opinions and fosters a resulting increase in the strength and rigor of one's own opinions and stances. As such, it helps readers assume their rightful place in the public square and provides them with the skills necessary to uphold their awesome responsibility—guaranteeing the continued and future health of a vital, vibrant, and free democracy.

Introduction

> *"If one thing is clear from studying breakdowns throughout history, it's that extreme polarization can kill democracies."*
>
> *Steven Levitsky and Daniel Ziblatt,* How Democracies Die

Political speech and behavior—as well as political systems—are often viewed in terms of a broad continuum from stability and consensus on the one hand to extremism and disorder on the other. Throughout much of the late twentieth century, the United States demonstrated considerable political stability as well as widespread intellectual consensus around certain fundamental principles and strategic imperatives. American democratic institutions were widely viewed as legitimate and reliable, and the country stood as a beacon of liberal democratic freedom for much of the world.

Since the 1980s, however, American politics has gradually become much more extremist and confrontational, and much less oriented toward moderate consensus. In their influential book *How Democracies Die*, Steven Levitsky and Daniel Ziblatt offer the following:

> The guardrails of American democracy are weakening. The erosion of our democratic norms began in the 1980s and 1990s and accelerated in the 2000s. By the time Barack Obama became president, many Republicans in particular questioned the legitimacy of their Democratic rivals and had abandoned

forbearance for a strategy of winning by any means necessary. Trump may have accelerated this process, but he didn't cause it. The challenges facing American democracy run deeper. The weakening of our democratic norms is rooted in extreme partisan polarization—one that extends beyond policy differences into an existential conflict over race and culture. America's efforts to achieve racial equality as our society grows increasingly diverse have fueled an insidious reaction and intensifying polarization.[1]

Levitsky and Ziblatt's analysis exemplifies a body of concerns that observers of American politics have been raising for the past several years. American newspapers and journals, as well as online forums, have become daily spaces of debate about what went wrong with American politics and why.

Some critics have focused on the role of our major political parties in fomenting a more hostile and polarized political atmosphere. The existence of parties in general in a democratic system tends to encourage an "us vs. them" / in-group vs. out-group framework for political issues. Moreover, the recent emergence and increased prominence of elected officials like former president Trump and Rep. Marjorie Taylor Greene on the right, and Senator Bernie Sanders and Rep. Alexandria Ocasio-Cortez on the left has contributed to perceptions of growing extremism. Consider the following, from an analysis published by researchers at the Pew Center:

> The divisions between Republicans and Democrats on fundamental political values—on government, race, immigration, national security, environmental protection and other areas—reached record levels during Barack Obama's presidency. In Donald Trump's first year as president, these gaps have grown even larger. And the magnitude of these differences dwarfs other divisions in society, along such lines as gender, race and ethnicity, religious observance or education. A new study by Pew Research Center, based on surveys of more than 5,000 adults conducted over the summer, finds widening differences between Republicans and Democrats on a range of measures the Center has been asking about since 1994, as well as

those with more recent trends. But in recent years, the gaps on several sets of political values in particular—including measures of attitudes about the social safety net, race and immigration—have increased dramatically.[2]

But the United States has seen extremist demagogues (e.g., George Wallace, Joseph McCarthy, etc.) in the past, and our political divisions have been growing wider for some time. This has motivated many political observers to look outside the party structure for the deep roots of today's growing extremism.

Some have pointed to the influence of a rapidly changing media environment. In the middle of the twentieth century, most Americans received their news from local papers and/or from a small handful of national broadcasters. These sources, because they assumed they were communicating with a mass audience, were careful to avoid ideological bias in their coverage. But during the 1980s and 1990s, Congress significantly deregulated the American media industries (e.g., the repeal of the 1987 Fairness Doctrine and the 1996 Telecommunications Act), which supercharged the growth of cable programming and opened the door to the type of partisan news coverage that is now familiar on Fox News and MSNBC.[3] The advent of the internet and social media further diversified the media and information environment in the United States and enabled the growth of what some critics refer to as "partisan echo chambers." Whether or not the media environment is responsible for the political divisions in our society, it has certainly accelerated their entrenchment and enabled extremist elements to promote their ideologies more efficiently.

The authors of the viewpoints in the following pages of *Current Controversies: Domestic Extremism* seek to explore the conditions that brought the country to where it is today and project what the future might look like. Despite the various perspectives on what causes extremism and what has fueled its spread in the United States, there is wide agreement among those who study democratic politics that the growth of extremism and polarization are among the most important and consequential political dynamics in American politics today. The next several years will offer an important test for the strength of American democracy.

Endnotes

1. "This Is How Democracies Die," by Steven Levitsky and Daniel Ziblatt, *Guardian*, January 21, 2018, https://www.theguardian.com/us-news /commentisfree/2018/jan/21/this-is-how-democracies-die.

2. "The Partisan Divide on Political Values Grows Even Wider," Pew Research Center, October 5, 2017, https://www.pewresearch.org/politics/2017/10/05 /the-partisan-divide-on-political-values-grows-even-wider/.

3. "The US Media's Problems Are Much Bigger Than Fake News and Filter Bubbles," by Bharat N. Anand, *Harvard Business Review*, January 5, 2017, https://hbr.org/2017/01/the-u-s-medias-problems-are-much-bigger-than-fake -news-and-filter-bubbles.

CHAPTER 1

Do Political Parties Encourage Extremism in the US?

Overview: The Impact of Political Parties on Democratic Governance

Didi Kuo

Didi Kuo is associate director for research at the Center on Democracy, Development, and the Rule of Law at Stanford University. She is also an affiliate of the Project on Global Populisms at the Freeman-Spogli Institute for International Studies.

Does democracy require parties, and if so, what are the consequences of weaker parties on democratic governance? At its simplest, democracy is a set of formal institutions and rules that govern how citizens select leaders and hold them to account. The relationship between citizens and government, however, is indirect. Representative democracy relies on parties to do most of the work of organizing politics. Parties groom and select candidates for office, coordinate election campaigns, and mobilize and educate voters. They also respond to voters' needs by devising and passing policies, through deliberation and consensus.

The history of representative democracy is inextricably intertwined with that of parties. In the United States, the founders were wary of parties but were unsuccessful in keeping parties out of national politics. Proto-party factions predated mass suffrage in many countries of western Europe, and became the primary vehicle to integrate citizens into democratic politics. In many other regions of the world, party building has been a challenging and critical component of democratic transition itself. Strong parties serve democracy, and there has long been a relationship between robust, stable party systems and successful democratic[20] and economic[21] outcomes.

"Challenges to Parties in the United States and Beyond," by Didi Kuo, New America. https://www.newamerica.org/political-reform/reports/political-parties-good-for /challenges-to-parties-in-the-united-states-and-beyond/. Licensed under CC BY-4.0.

Inside and outside the United States, parties continue to be central to democracy. They command significant financial resources, have become more ideologically cohesive, and, of course, continue to win elections. Money and partisanship, however, do not make for strong parties. As Julia Azari has written, what makes today's politics so volatile is the precise combination of weak parties and strong partisanship.[22]

This series of essays for Polyarchy shows that parties have weakened over time in two respects. The first is that they no longer perform as significant a role as gatekeepers in the political process, particularly over candidate selection. Changes to the party nomination process, combined with new communications technologies, make it easier for candidates to run outside the party system.

Second, parties' capacity to respond to the needs of voters has declined. The erosion of local parties, civic associations, and trade unions makes it harder for parties to maintain connections to voters. Parties also shifted their bases of support in the late twentieth century away from working-class interests toward more educated and affluent interests.

After the "third way" politics of the 1990s, parties came to broad agreement over many aspects of economic policy. On areas as varied as trade, welfare austerity, and corporate and financial regulation, parties embraced, to varying degrees, neoliberal approaches. The narrowed space for policy contestation led the noted political scientist Peter Mair to lament that[23] "the age of party democracy has passed."

The implications of these changes—of less party gatekeeping and less responsiveness—are significant. When parties perform their duties effectively, they integrate citizens into politics,[24] keep radical candidates out of power,[25] and negotiate between[26] competing powerful interests. As these essays make clear, however, there are real concerns about the role of parties today. Weaker parties have significant consequences: They make democracy more vulnerable to instability, backsliding, and insurgent candidates.

Further, distrust in parties makes it harder for citizens to understand the value of democracy itself, since parties are a crucial vehicle for citizen mobilization and education. When parties are not responsive to the demands of citizens, they make it more likely that citizens will find fault with all of democratic government, rather than simply with parties themselves.

The Decline of Trust in Parties

Parties have long been considered imperfect vehicles of democracy. In the early years of the American republic, the founders decried the perils of faction. George Washington warned of the "baneful effects" and "constant danger" of parties in his farewell address, arguing that they served to inflame anger and jealousy, or as conduits of corruption. Centuries later, Dwight D. Eisenhower claimed that unless parties advanced "a cause that is right and that is moral," it is not a party at all—only a "conspiracy to seize power."

Citizens now report record levels of distrust in parties as part of a slow decline in trust in government more generally. Fewer than 20 percent[27] of Americans report that they can trust the government to do what is right most of the time. After the federal government shutdown of 2013, trust in Congress plummeted to a mere 7 percent, although it has been low since the financial crisis.

While these trends parallel a decline in trust across institutions, including the media, big business, and organized religion, they also relate to partisanship. Republicans are more likely to trust government when their party is in power, and less likely to trust it when out of power; the same is true for Democrats.

Parties have also become more ideologically cohesive in the United States. While this kind of polarization is often useful in helping voters identify a clear party of the left and right, partisanship today has resulted not in more trust in parties, but more antipathy. Political rhetoric has grown more hostile, and negotiation and compromise between the parties seems, at times, impossible. Among voters, partisans increasingly map their social identities onto their partisan ones. As a result, Liliana Mason finds that Democratic and Republican voters are less willing to accept compromise.

Intense partisans stand in contrast to those who feel turned off by partisanship. Voters identifying as independents now outnumber those who identify as Republicans or Democrats, and the share of independents in the electorate has been rising steadily. What are the effects of these trends in party identification? In a study of self-identified independents,[28] Samara Klar and Yanna Krupnikov show that while some independent voters may lean toward one of the main parties, they are not reliable partisans. Instead, they are likely to be alienated from parties and politics and to be more concerned with, say, corruption than with policy issues, such as the economy or health care.

Unease with parties is not limited to the United States. In western European countries, where party membership is often formalized—party members pay dues and receive formal party benefits—partisan voters are also on the decline. Party membership has been reduced by nearly half[29] since 1980; this trend is particularly pronounced in the Nordic countries, France, Italy, and Britain. Party members' educational and professional backgrounds are similar to those of party elites, and party members are also more likely to work in the public sector than non-party members; they are not representative[30] of the broader population. Sheri Berman's history of social democratic parties[31] shows how these parties have pivoted away from the organizational forms that once defined them.

Voters' ambivalence towards established parties is often attributed to changes beyond the scope of domestic politics. Globalization, economic inequality, declines in manufacturing, immigration, and a new assertiveness among illiberal leaders all play a role in voter discontent. However, in this period, party organizations themselves have remained robust. Parties run sophisticated operations with large paid staff, professional party elites, and a network of affiliated public relations and marketing firms. Parties maintain sophisticated databases of their supporters; there is an industry of firms that help with outreach and mobilization. This prioritization of electoral strategy has traded off, however, with parties' ability to serve as gatekeepers, and to respond to the needs of voters.

Gatekeeping

One reason for the robust empirical relationship between strong parties and stable democracy is related to the important role that parties perform as gatekeepers. Party leaders have a stake in the longevity of the party itself, rather than any individual politician. Because democracy is a repeated game, party leaders have incentives to sustain party organizations across successive elections. Political parties therefore function as gatekeepers in the democratic process, keeping radical candidates and ideas out of mainstream politics. Daniel Ziblatt's history of conservative parties[32] in Europe found that strong parties—those with salaried professionals and widespread local associations—were able to contain reactionary forces, while weak parties were instead susceptible to them.

Candidates in the United States and Europe almost always run under the banner of a party, and party leaders tend to support candidates who have a chance of winning. This has often entailed choosing moderates over extremists. However, the candidate selection process has become distorted by a number of factors.

First, American and European parties have adopted more internal democracy, letting members choose candidates instead of relying on party elites alone. This has undermined the traditional role of party elites in candidate selection, and it is this plebiscitary trend,[33] according to Frances Rosenbluth and Ian Shapiro, that makes it impossible for party leaders to form consensus over nominees and policies.

In *How Democracies Die*,[34] Ziblatt and Levitsky lay the blame for the rise of political outsiders squarely on the inability of parties to manage candidate selection. Daniel Schlozman and

Sam Rosenfeld's history of the Democratic Party[35] shows how the McGovern-Fraser reformers sought to wrest control of the party from a small group of party bosses, which led voters to make greater participation synonymous with legitimacy.

Another challenge to gatekeeping is money in politics. Parties used to have more control over financing of campaigns and party activities. The world of campaign finance, however, has become more diffuse. The Bipartisan Campaign Finance Reform Act limited the soft money parties could raise and use, and a series of Supreme Court decisions protects political money as a constitutional right.

There are debates about what this means for parties. While there is some evidence[36] that states that allow parties greater control over financing elect more moderate politicians, others argue that the diffuse world of finance is simply an extension of party[37] control. Regardless, candidates for office now face a set of stakeholders and donors beyond their own parties and constituencies. Outside groups can also perform many of the duties once left to parties, including campaign advertising and get-out-the-vote efforts.

A final challenge to gatekeeping has to do with technology and the ease with which outsiders can connect with voters. The internet and social media provide individual candidates with cheap forms of outreach, circumventing traditional ways of coming up through the party system. The Five Star party in Italy, which has the most seats in Parliament, began as an internet party.

These new candidates are not always extremists; Emmanuel Macron's La République En Marche was a new party, as was the party of Slovakia's new president, the activist and reformer Zuzana Caputova. In March, the Ukrainian actor Volodymyr Zelensky won the presidency; much of his campaign was organized online. Donald Trump, already a celebrity in his own right, relied (and continues to rely) heavily on direct communication with voters through Twitter. Technology reduces the barriers to entry for new politicians who can outflank parties, therefore undermining the ability of parties to claim they are necessary gatekeepers in politics.

Responsiveness

In addition to playing less of an important role as gatekeepers, parties also do not serve the representative functions that they once did. Historically, parties were created to represent distinct interests among citizens—working-class and labor interests, landowning and business interests, rural and urban constituencies, etc. Not only did they sustain ties to these groups at the local level, but they also reflected these interests in the policies they pursued. Both of these mechanisms of responsiveness have eroded, as parties focus increasingly on professional services and national elections, and as many areas of policy have been removed from the legislative arena.

As Berman argues, social democratic parties were once embedded in the quotidian lives of voters: They provided educational and job opportunities, scholarships, and leisure activities. Parties were organizing principles for local communities. And while the United States does not have a history of social democratic parties, American parties used to be much more robust networks of state and local organizations. These mid-century parties institutionalized relationships with professional and civic associations.

The decline of unions and civic associations has therefore had a profound impact on parties across the advanced industrial nations. In the United States, a proliferation in right-to-work laws across conservative states has had the effect of reducing[38] both the vote share and labor contributions to Democrats. Union membership is also associated with greater representation[39] of working-class interests in policy.

Finally, policymaking itself has changed. Many policy issues fall outside the scope of public deliberation and contestation, which leaves parties with few ways to demonstrate responsiveness in the form of policy. The European Union makes decisions about trade, migration, and economic policy that affect its member states, but its connection to domestic voters is highly attenuated.

Ironically, the European Union has indirectly assisted the rise of new parties (particularly on the far right), which emerged to compete in elections to the European Parliament. In the

2014 European parliamentary elections, the UK Independence Party won more seats than the Conservative or Labour parties; the far-right Alternative for Germany and Swedish Democrats and the populist-left Podemos party in Spain also won seats that year. Parties in the European Parliament receive financing and party-building resources that they can use to influence national elections.

While no similar dynamic exists in the United States, the scope of policymaking has nonetheless contracted due to centrist politics that produced greater consensus over economic and social policy between the parties. In the 1990s, center-left parties in the United States and western Europe embraced lowered trade barriers, greater financial integration, welfare retrenchment, deregulation, and privatization. Lily Geismer traces the roots of this Democratic move to the right, showing how a new generation of Democrats embraced neoliberalism[40] and mobilized educated, urban professionals. When the ideological distinctions between parties become blurred, voters are more likely to reject[41] parties altogether.

Thirty years ago, the Italian political scientist Angelo Panebianco described a future of "electoral-professional parties"[42] that outsourced candidate selection and policy to interest groups and bureaucrats, while focusing on services (such as advertising and polling) for candidates. This represented a dramatic shift from the mass organizational parties that served critical functions of gatekeeping and representation in politics. Today, the foremost theory[43] of American parties concedes this basic premise, describing parties as mere groups of policy demanders rather than robust organizations that connect citizens to their governments.

But the rich history of parties both in and outside the United States tells us that successful democratic outcomes are dependent on the strength of parties. These parties need institutionalized mechanisms to absorb citizen demands, and need to use the levers of policy to respond. Further, they need greater control over aspects of representative government—including the cultivation and selection of candidates, and the ability to negotiate and compromise—that voters feel are increasingly broken.

Although it is hard to see how we might go back to the organizationally dense parties of the mid-century, party reformers must prioritize shoring up the capacities of parties in order to forestall greater public disaffection with democracy.

Endnotes

20. Scott Mainwaring and Timothy R. Scully, *Building Democratic Institutions: Party Systems in Latin America* (Palo Alto, CA: Stanford University Press, 1995).

21. Fernando Bizzarro, John Gerring, and Carl Henrik Hudson et al., "Party Strength and Economic Growth," *World Politics* 70(2) (April 2018): 275–320.

22. Julia Azari, "Weak parties and strong partisanship are a bad combination," *Vox*, November 3, 2016, https://www.vox.com/mischiefs -of-faction/2016/11/3/13512362/weak-parties-strong-partisanship-bad -combination

23. Peter Mair, *Ruling the Void: The Hollowing of Western Democracies* (London: Verso, 2013).

24. Nancy L. Rosenblum, *On the Side of Angels: An Appreciation of Parties and Partisanship* (Princeton, NJ: Princeton University Press, 2008).

25. Daniel Ziblatt, *Conservative Parties and the Birth of Democracy* (Cambridge, UK: Cambridge University Press, 2017).

26. Nathaniel Persily, *Solutions to Political Polarization in America* (New York: Cambridge University Press, 2015).

27. Pew Research Center, *Public Trust in Government 1958-2019* (Washington, DC: Pew Research Center, April 2019).

28. Samara Klarr, *Independent Politics: How American Disdain for Parties Leads to Political Inaction* (Cambridge, UK: Cambridge University Press, 2016).

29. Ingrid Van Biezen, Peter Mair, Thomas Poguntke, "Going, going...gone? The decline of part membership in contemporary Europe," *European Journal of Political Research* 51(1) (May 2011): 24–56. https://doi.org/10.1111/j.1475 -6765.2011.01995.x

30. Susan Scarrow, *Beyond Party Members: Changing Approaches to Partisan Mobilization* (Oxford, UK: Oxford University Press, 2015).

31. Sheri Berman, "The development and decay of democracy," *Vox*, June 18, 2019, https:// www.vox.com/polyarchy/2019/6/18/18679260/social-democracy -development-decay

32. Daniel Ziblatt, *Conservative Parties and the Birth of Democracy* (Cambridge, UK: Cambridge University Press, 2017).

33. Frances Rosenbluth and Ian Shapiro, *Responsible Parties: Saving Democracy from Itself* (New Haven, CT: Yale University Press, 2018).

34. Steven Levitsky and Daniel Ziblatt, *How Democracies Die* (New York: Broadway Books, 2019).

35. Sam Rosenfeld and Daniel Schlozman, "The dilemmas for Democrats in 3 past visions for the party," *Vox*, June 13, 2019.

36. Raymond J. La Raja and Brian F. Schaffner, *Campaign Finance and Political Polarization: When Purists Prevail* (Ann Arbor, MI: University of Michigan Press, 2015).

37. Thomas E. Mann and Anthony Corrado, *Party Polarization and Campaign Finance* (Washington, DC: Brookings, 2014). https://www.brookings.edu /wp-content/uploads/2016/06/Mann-and-Corrad_Party-Polarization-and -Campaign-Finance.pdf

38. James Feigenbaum, Alexander Hertel-Fernandez, and Vanessa Williamson, *From the Bargaining Table to the Ballot Box: Political Effects of Right to Work Laws* (Washington, DC: The National Bureau of Economic Research, 2018), https://www.nber.org/papers/w24259

39. Patrick Falvin, "Labor Union Strength and the Equality of Political Representation," *British Journal of Political Science* 48(4) (October 2018) 1075–1091. https://doi.org/10.1017/S0007123416000302

40. Lily Geismer, "Democrats and neoliberalism," *Vox*, June 11, 2019, https://www .vox.com/polyarchy/2019/6/11/18660240/democrats-neoliberalism

41. Noam Lupu, *Party Brands in Crisis: Partisanship, Brand Dilution, and the Breakdown of Political Parties in Latin America* (Cambridge, UK: Cambridge University Press, 2015).

42. Angelo Banebianco, *Political Parties: Organization and Power* (Cambridge, UK: Cambridge University Press, 2003).

43. Kathleen Bawn, Martin Cohen, David Karol, Seth Masket, Hans Noel, and John Zaller, "A Theory of Political Parties: Groups, Policy Demands and Nominations in American Politics," *Perspectives on Politics* 10(3) (September 2012): 571–597, doi:10.1017/ S1537592712001624

The Rise of Negative Partisanship in American Politics

Alexis Blue

Alexis Blue is director of news content and communications at the University of Arizona and editor of the UANow *newsletter. She is a senior writer for UA publications, covering topics in psychology, family and consumer sciences, and social science.*

Democrats and Republicans are about as warm toward their own political parties as they were decades ago, but their dislike for the opposition has significantly increased, says UArizona political scientist Chris Weber.

It's become a familiar refrain in the months and weeks leading up to Nov. 3: "This is the most important election of our lifetimes."

It's not the first time such a claim has been made, but Americans on both ends of the political spectrum seem especially keen to embrace it amid this year's contentious presidential race.

Most voters already know who will get their vote when they head to polls in a couple of weeks; many have already cast their votes via mail-in ballot. But what might be even clearer to voters when it comes to this year's presidential race is the person they don't want as their commander-in-chief.

The tendency to support a political party or candidate based primarily on dislike for the "other side" is known as negative partisanship, and it's been picking up steam in American politics, says a University of Arizona political scientist.

"Negative partisanship is the idea that people choose a party not necessarily based on the party's platform or even the candidate. They do so out of animosity or dislike or disdain toward the opposing party," said Chris Weber, an associate professor in the

"Political Scientist Describes the Rise of Negative Partisanship and How It Drives Voters," by Alexis Blue, October 21, 2020 Copyright © 2020 The University of Arizona, Reprinted by Permission. https://news.arizona.edu/story/rise-negative-partisanship-and-how-it-drives-voters.

School of Government and Public Policy in the College of Social and Behavioral Sciences.

It's why your social media feeds may seem more filled with impassioned pleas to vote against a particular candidate than cases made in favor of the alternative.

The concept of negative partisanship isn't new, but it's intensified as American politics have grown more polarized, says Weber, who researches voter behavior and psychology.

"Since the early '90s or so, political parties started to grow really polarized, meaning the Republican Party grew more conservative and the Democratic Party grew more liberal," Weber said.

While research has shown that Republican politicians' shift to the right has been far more pronounced than Democrats' shift to the left, it's fair to say that both parties have moved farther away from one another, ideologically, Weber said. And although this hasn't generally changed how voters feel about their own political party of choice, it's certainly stoked negative feelings toward the opposition.

"If we use what's called a feeling thermometer, which is commonly used in the political science literature, and you ask voters on a scale of zero to 100 how warm they feel toward a political party, those who are Republican are about as warm toward Republicans now as Republicans were 30 to 40 years ago, and the same holds true for Democrats, on average," Weber said. "What's changed is the striking dip in feelings toward the opposing party, so Democrats are much more cold toward Republicans and Republicans are much more cold toward Democrats."

Is that "cold" sentiment enough to get people to the polls, even in cases when they might not feel an equal degree of enthusiasm for their own party's candidate? Yes, Weber says.

"One consequence of anger, and even negative campaigning in certain circumstances, is that it actually does increase voter turnout," Weber said. "I'm not going to claim that that's what we should desire or hope for, but it is a consequence. So, this idea that you can really stoke fear or anxiety to turn up the base has actually been empirically shown to be true."

High voter turnout aside, the animosity that accompanies negative partisanship is far from a positive thing, Weber says.

"Viewing half of the country or a large section of the country as antithetical to American democracy is actually really harmful," he said. "These are neighbors in many cases. So, I would certainly not call it a good or desirable thing. It's a deleterious characteristic of modern democracy, and it's an outgrowth of political polarization that has potentially very serious consequences."

The changing media landscape over the last couple of decades has also contributed to negative partisanship, Weber said, as people have been given more power to pick and choose news sources that align with their viewpoints and might not offer balanced or even credible information.

"People can now put themselves in these information environments where their beliefs aren't really challenged, and we as Americans are not necessarily exposing ourselves to a common set of information or common media platform anymore, which certainly doesn't help," he said.

Weber says that as political parties have become less ideologically diverse internally—with fewer members of both major parties leaning more toward the center—there starts to be a "falling out of the middle" that has the potential to erode civil behavior and the ability for people to negotiate and find common ground.

Not all hope is lost, however. There are things that can be done to combat negative partisanship, Weber says.

"The more people pay attention to and try to appreciate points of view they don't necessarily agree with (and) the extent to which politicians stop vilifying out-party candidates and actually speak to the issues at hand—these are solutions," he said.

Weber also notes that while negative partisanship has intensified in the bases of the Democratic and Republican parties, US voters who identify as independent outnumber those who say they are Democrats and those who say they are Republicans.

"That leaves a large segment of the population and their vote up for grabs," Weber said. "So, successful candidates will be not only those who appeal to their ideological base but also cater to the beliefs of the middle. There's so much perceived extremism now; I'm hopeful at some point the parties will start moving back to the middle again."

Is Partisanship Accelerating in the United States?

Pew Research Center

The Pew Research Center is a nonpartisan think tank that conducts opinion polling, demographic research, content analysis, and other data-driven social science research. Pew does not take policy positions and states that its primary objective is to generate a foundation of facts that enriches public dialogue and supports sound decision making.

The divisions between Republicans and Democrats on fundamental political values—on government, race, immigration, national security, environmental protection and other areas—reached record levels during Barack Obama's presidency. In Donald Trump's first year as president, these gaps have grown even larger.

And the magnitude of these differences dwarfs other divisions in society, along such lines as gender, race and ethnicity, religious observance or education.

A new study by Pew Research Center, based on surveys of more than 5,000 adults conducted over the summer, finds widening differences between Republicans and Democrats on a range of measures the Center has been asking about since 1994, as well as those with more recent trends. But in recent years, the gaps on several sets of political values in particular—including measures of attitudes about the social safety net, race and immigration—have increased dramatically.

Government Aid to Needy

Over the past six years, the share of Democrats and Democratic-leaning independents saying the government should do more

"The Partisan Divide on Political Values Grows Even Wider," Pew Research Center, October 5, 2017. Reprinted by permission.

to help the needy, even if it means going deeper into debt, has risen 17 percentage points (from 54% to 71%), while the views of Republicans and Republican leaners have barely changed (25% then, 24% today). However, Republicans' opinions on this issue had shifted substantially between 2007 and 2011, with the share favoring more aid to the needy falling 20 points (from 45% to 25%).

The result: While there has been a consistent party gap since 1994 on government aid to the poor, the divisions have never been this large. In 2011, about twice as many Democrats as Republicans said the government should do more for the needy (54% vs. 25%). Today, nearly three times as many Democrats as Republicans say this (71% vs. 24%).

Racial Discrimination

In recent years, Democrats' views on racial discrimination also have changed, driving an overall shift in public opinion. Currently, 41% of Americans say racial discrimination is the main reason many blacks cannot get ahead—the largest share expressing this view in surveys dating back 23 years. Still, somewhat more Americans (49%) say blacks who cannot get ahead are mostly responsible for their own condition.

When the racial discrimination question was first asked in 1994, the partisan difference was 13 points. By 2009, it was only somewhat larger (19 points). But today, the gap in opinions between Republicans and Democrats about racial discrimination and black advancement has increased to 50 points.

Immigration

Nearly two-thirds of Americans (65%) say immigrants strengthen the country "because of their hard work and talents." Just 26% say immigrants are a burden "because they take our jobs, housing and health care." Views of immigrants, though little changed from a year ago, are more positive than at any point in the past two decades.

As with views of racial discrimination, there has been a major shift in Democrats' opinions about immigrants. The share of Democrats who say immigrants strengthen the country has increased from 32% in 1994 to 84% today. By contrast, Republicans are divided in attitudes about immigrants: 42% say they strengthen the country, while 44% view them as a burden. In 1994, 30% of Republicans said immigrants strengthened the country, while 64% said they were a burden.

"Peace Through Strength"

About six-in-ten Americans (61%) say good diplomacy is the best way to ensure peace, while 30% say peace is ensured by military strength. Opinions in both parties have changed since the 1990s; Democrats increasingly say peace is ensured by good diplomacy, while Republicans say it is military strength that ensures peace. Today, 83% of Democrats and Democratic leaners see good diplomacy as the way to ensure peace, compared with just 33% of Republicans and Republican leaners.

The surveys were conducted June 8–18 among 2,504 adults and June 27–July 9 among 2,505 adults, with a follow-up survey conducted Aug. 15–21 among 1,893 respondents. This report was made possible by The Pew Charitable Trusts, which received support for the surveys from The William and Flora Hewlett Foundation.

Party Gaps Much Larger Than Demographic Differences

The partisan shifts on political values over the past 23 years have had different trajectories across different sets of issues. While there has been greater movement among Democrats than Republicans on several issues, on others Republicans have shown more change.

In views of stricter environmental laws and regulations, for example, there has been a larger long-term change among Republicans than Democrats. Republicans are far less supportive of stricter environmental laws than they were in the mid-1990s, while Democrats have become somewhat more supportive.

But the bottom line is this: Across 10 measures that Pew Research Center has tracked on the same surveys since 1994, the average partisan gap has increased from 15 percentage points to 36 points.

Two decades ago, the average partisan differences on these items were only somewhat wider than differences by religious attendance or educational attainment and about as wide as the differences between blacks and whites (14 points, on average). Today, the party divide is much wider than any of these demographic differences.

Partisan gaps have grown even on measures in which opinion in both parties has moved in the same direction, such as support for societal acceptance of homosexuality. Currently, 70% of Americans say homosexuality should be accepted—the highest percentage ever.

For the first time, a majority of Republicans (54%) favor acceptance of homosexuality; just 38% did so in 1994. Yet over this period, the increase in the share of Democrats saying homosexuality should be accepted has been much larger (from 54% to 83%). As a result, partisan differences have gotten larger.

The surveys find that while Republicans and Democrats have grown further apart, there are sizable divisions within both parties on many political values. Younger Republicans differ from older Republicans in attitudes about immigration and several other issues. Among Republicans and Republican leaners younger than 30, 62% say immigrants strengthen the country; half as many Republicans ages 65 and older say the same (31%).

In recent years, there has been a decline in the share of Democrats who say that most people can get ahead if they work hard. Only about half of Democrats (49%) express this view, down from 58% three years ago. A large majority of Republicans (77%) continue to say hard work pays off for most people.

Democrats are divided by education and race in their views of hard work and success. White Democrats and those with higher levels of education are less likely than nonwhite Democrats and those with less education to say that hard work leads to success.

Other Important Findings

Partisan Antipathy Remains Extensive

The shares of Republicans and Democrats who express *very* unfavorable opinions of the opposing party have increased dramatically since the 1990s, but have changed little in recent years. Currently, 44% of Democrats and Democratic leaners have a very unfavorable opinion of the GOP, based on yearly averages of Pew Research Center surveys; 45% of Republicans and Republican leaners view the Democratic Party very unfavorably. In 1994, fewer than 20% in both parties viewed the opposing party very unfavorably.

Big House, Small House

Our studies of political polarization and partisan antipathy both found that the disagreements between Republicans and Democrats go far beyond political values and issues. They also have markedly different preferences about where they would like to live. Most Republicans (65%) say they would rather live in a community where houses are larger and farther apart and where schools and shopping are not nearby. A majority of Democrats (61%) prefer smaller houses within walking distance of schools and shopping.

Deep Differences over Factors for Nation's Success

About half of Americans (52%) attribute the country's success more to "its ability to change," while 43% say the nation's "reliance on long-standing principles" has been more important. Most Democrats (68%) link the nation's success more to its ability to change, while 61% of Republicans point to its reliance on principles. In addition, there are wide age differences, with young people far more likely than older adults to say America's success is mainly linked to its ability to change.

Parties Are a Defining Element of Representative Democracy

Russell Muirhead and Nancy L. Rosenblum

Russell Muirhead is the Robert Clements Professor of Democracy and Politics at Dartmouth College. His work focuses on democratic theory and on ideas and institutions in American constitutional democracy. Nancy Rosenblum is Senator Joseph S. Clark Professor of Ethics in Politics and Government at Harvard University and co-editor of the Annual Review of Political Science. *Her work focuses on ethics, democratic theory, and constitutional law.*

In political science, parties are a defining element of representative democracy; as Schattschneider (1942, p. 1) wrote in *Party Government*, "political parties created democracy and…modern democracy is unthinkable save in terms of parties." Yet, until recently, a chasm existed between political science and normative democratic theory, which was silent on parties and partisanship.

A vast literature in empirical political science covers party systems, the function and dysfunction of political parties, campaigns and elections, partisan identity, and much more. In recent work on democracies in crisis, parties again occupy a central place (Cain 2015, Rosenbluth & Shapiro 2018). Strong parties and party systems are "democracy's gatekeepers" (Levitsky & Ziblatt 2018, p. 20), vital for democratic legitimacy and stability. Many political scientists worry that political parties, "once the primary instruments for combining democracy's positive virtues," are at risk (Runciman 2018, p. 214).

Despite their centrality to modern democracy, parties have been "the orphans of political philosophy," as Schattschneider (1942, p. 16) put it more than 75 years ago. They remained at the

"The Political Theory of Parties and Partisanship: Catching Up," by Russell Muirhead and Nancy L. Rosenblum, *Annual Reviews*, May 2020. https://www.annualreviews.org/doi /full/10.1146/annurev-polisci-041916-020727. Licensed under CC BY-4.0 International.

margins of normative democratic theory, if they appeared at all. They have been largely absent from agonistic, liberal, deliberative, and participatory democratic theories. There is a strong tendency in normative theory to view parties as corrupt and corrupting; as factions ambitious to exercise power; as unreasonable, unrepresentative, and undemocratic. Democratic theorists have entertained dispensing with both parties and elections altogether (Guerrero 2014). They have focused instead on the democratic value of social movements, civil society associations, deliberative experiments, spaces for local participatory government, and direct popular participation—referenda and initiatives (Fung 2012).

Our subject here is the political theory of party and partisanship as it has arisen—one might say finally—in the last 15 years. A normative literature on parties and partisanship has developed, as theorists have begun to assign parties (and, to a significantly lesser extent, partisanship) a place in democratic theory. They invest parties with normative content. And they turn the tables, pointing out the consequences of a paucity of normative standards in the empirical literature (White & Ypi 2016, pp. 10–20; Herman 2017). Today, the distance separating empirical accounts of parties and their normative status is less stark, and increasing numbers of political theorists insist that democratic theorists and party scholars should talk to each other (van Biezen & Saward 2008, Bonotti & Bader 2015). Our subject is the burgeoning literature in democratic theory that focuses directly on parties and partisanship.

Our first section below assesses the literature on parties and representation. In the second section, we turn to a central theme: the normative defense of parties. One thread of defense argues that parties play a special role in political justification as agents of public reason. A related thread sees parties as contributors to deliberation. A third thread prizes their commitment to regulated political rivalry and peaceful rotation in office. In this connection, we survey work on the constitutional status of parties and reasons for banning parties. In the third section, our focus shifts from parties to partisanship and its relation to citizenship, and in a fourth section we turn to the ethics of partisanship. This organization indicates that parties and partisanship are interwoven but separable topics in political theory. A defense of parties often comes with a depreciation of partisanship, but partisanship too has defenders. If partisans are necessary to realize the value of parties, the reverse holds as well, and parties are necessary to realize the value of partisanship.

Running through this review is our identification of three normative foundations of political parties. One is the value of dynamic political pluralism—diversity of opinion, experience, interest, and identity. The second is the value of institutionalizing pluralism in organized parties for the purposes of politics and governing. The third is the place of parties in acknowledging a legitimate opposition and commitment to peaceful rotation in office. We note where democratic theorists take account of these fundamentals or disregard them, and at what cost. The cost of disregard can be high, for historically (and still today) assaults on parties and partisanship are a principal way of assaulting democracy. Invariably, these assaults take the form of antipathy to pluralism, rejection of parties as a vital framework of pluralism in democratic politics, and insistence that the opposition is not a loyal opposition but a conspiracy against the public good. This is the malignant trio behind antipartyism today. In conclusion we ask, do theorists attend to these mounting forces? Does their work enable us to recognize and address the present danger head on?

Parties and Representation (The Partisan Connection)

Canonical work in the history of political thought recognized the role of parties (or proto-parties) in political representation. An abbreviated list of such thinkers includes Machiavelli, who saw in the Roman contest of plebs and elites a dynamic opposition that could function to stabilize a regime (McCormick 2011). David Hume appreciated parties in a similar fashion, and against the republican insistence on sameness—enforced through sumptuary laws and a static economy—saw parties as an inevitable and acceptable part of freedom and commercial society (Sabl 2012, Landis 2017). In the late eighteenth century, Edmund Burke's defense of partisanship was more explicit than his predecessors', which is why some see him as the founder not only of modern conservatism but of modern partisanship (Mansfield 1965). What stands out especially is his famous contrast of delegate and trustee models of representation. Some interpreters see a defense of party even in the writings of Madison, who, though he warned about faction, helped found the first American opposition party as the representative of republicanism (Connolly 2011). Recent work on eighteenth- and nineteenth-century parliamentarism shows how a variety of thinkers, including Burke and Germaine de Staël, believed that the bond of partisan attachment among representatives "moderated the corrupting effect of patronage" (Selinger 2019, p. 72). Scholars of the history of political thought have interpreted and mined these writers and others, paying attention to the theme of representation. Yet, until recently, contemporary political theory did not follow suit.

Four decades ago, Stokes (1968, p. 152) wrote that although "parties and party systems have played an immensely important role in developing the public's control of leaders and conferring legitimacy on the regime," theorists rarely connect parties to "the concept of representation." In Pitkin's (1967, pp. 147–48) classic account, *The Concept of Representation*, parties appear briefly and disappear quickly. Although, as Disch (2012, p. 605) argues, Pitkin's understanding of representation is more "radical" than many readers identified, Pitkin does not assign a central role to parties and partisans in the dynamic process by which representation is created. Hers is not the only account in which parties remain in the shadows—for in many innovative and compelling recent theories of representation, parties and partisanship remain absent (Guerrero 2010, Montanaro 2012).

Still, more theorists of representation are heeding the call for normative democratic theorists and party scholars to "talk to each other" (Van Biezen & Saward 2008) and recognize—sometimes with careful analysis, sometimes in passing—the central role of parties and partisanship in representation (Disch 2002, Urbinati & Warren 2008, Mansbridge 2011, Wampler 2012, Saward 2014). That said, in many instances, political representation is conceived of as a relationship between an individual citizen and an official representative, with party and partisanship playing a merely facilitative background role.

This image of a representative as bound to a constituency in some respects but independent in others is rooted in the nineteenth-century era of parliamentarism—which is the historical location where some ethical dilemmas of representation, such as Pitkin's "mandate-independence controversy," are most appropriately situated (Manin 1997; Selinger 2019, pp. 173–74). Parliamentarianism was characterized by a relationship of personal trust between citizens and their chosen representatives, who were distinguished by their "local connections, their social prominence, or by the deference they provoked" (Manin 1997, p. 202). The legislature was a discursive body in which individual representatives could deliberate together and make decisions independent of their constituents' wishes.

In Manin's (1997) much-cited theoretical account, the connection between parties and representation came with the advent of "party democracy" in the twentieth century. People came to vote for the party rather than the person, and party voting became an expression of class identity (Manin 1997, pp. 208–9). Yet a variety of social changes upset the alliance of class-based cleavages and parties, and by the late twentieth century, it became increasingly difficult to sustain the partisan connection linking the society and the state. This created a need to reconceptualize parties and their role in representation. In empirical political science, there is debate about whether parties are adequately understood as umbrellas or alliances of activists and policy demanders or whether they have a more active and sustained role in mediating between ordinary citizens, activists and policy demanders, and the state (McCarty & Schickler 2018). In both political science and political theory, the decline of party democracy is seen as a crisis of representation.

In Europe, the crisis takes the form of parties that have disengaged from society. As Mair (2013, p. 97) writes, "Parties have reduced their presence in the wider society and have become part of the state. They have become agencies that govern...rather than represent" (see also Ignazi 2018). And as parties have disengaged from society, they have become "neither liked nor trusted" (Mair 2013, p. 73). In the United States, ideologically indistinct parties of the mid-twentieth century did not quite fit Manin's (1997) model of party democracy, and the crisis of representation took a different form. Rather than becoming agents of the nonpartisan state, as in Europe, parties in the United States became more ideological and more polarized. This, combined with the paucity of choices offered in a two-party system, created a chasm between partisan elites and ordinary citizens (Disch 2002, Fiorina & Abrams 2011). Parties in the United States have been captured by "the most energized segments of the population [that] attempt to pull government policy to their own preferences" (Cohen et al. 2008, quoted by McCarty & Schickler 2018, p. 177). This disconnect has the same effect as what Mair describes for European parties; it severs the partisan connection between legislature and society (Fiorina & Abrams 2011, Gilens 2012, Achen & Bartels 2016).

Whether the disconnect between parties and society in fact constitutes a "crisis" of representation is open to interpretation, but it does constitute a failure of the elemental linkage function long attributed to parties. This failure sets the stage for current scholarship in political theory on representation, which sees it as not necessarily situated in formal elective offices, and more contestatory and dynamic. Manin (1997, p. 226) puts it this way: As social and class cleavages become more complicated, representatives have to "take the initiative in proposing a line of division"; they have to call to awareness "this or that social division, drawing attention to a split in society that was not previously apparent." Saward (2010) goes further: To represent is to make a "representative claim"—a claim that is open to argument and contestation—and he challenges the assumptions that government is the primary container of representation and that elected officials are the quintessential representatives. Representation is not a fact—it is an event (Saward 2010, p. 39), and the representative claim is made across society, inside and outside the formal realm of official politics, from nongovernmental organizations to advocacy groups to international organizations (Saward 2010, pp. 26–27; Urbinati 2006, pp. 40–44). In this view, political theorists should focus more on whom these groups and associations claim to represent, and how, and on who contests these claims.

It would be a mistake to categorize elected partisan representatives as one set among many who make a representative claim, however. Legislatures are distinctive because of the power vested in them, whether a supreme power, as the Westminster Parliament possesses in principle, or the circumscribed power of legislatures in federal systems or separation-of-powers constitutions. Either way, it is not the legislature as a whole but the largest group within it that rules. The goal of creating a group or a coalition large enough to rule is what causes parties to form, and this irrepressible goal is what makes parties inevitable wherever elected legislatures exist (Muirhead 2014).

Parties and partisans make a distinctive claim: that they seek to govern. This is why the crisis of political representation cannot be elided by multiplying the sites of representation or by attending to the variety of competing representative claims that different actors advance. If parties cannot link the groups vying for power in the legislature with groups in the larger society, then legislatures, which are the heart of representative government, lose their connection to popular interests, wants, and passions, and representative government loses something of its legitimacy. Parties are the institution that successfully democratized representative government, and neither political science nor political theory gives us reason to believe that after their demise a different, more democratic institution will replace them.

Defending Parties

Discussion of parties in normative theory only rarely focuses on representation and the institutional context of parties. Instead, a major thrust is a defense of parties for democracy and democratic practices broadly, and within this rubric are several strands of argument. We begin with the defense of parties rooted in political history and institutions. It focuses on the value of parties as nonviolent means of altering government and specifically on the commitment to regulated political rivalry and legitimate opposition. Two other strands of defense are rooted in political philosophy and identify the value of parties in effecting higher-level democratic ideals that are external to parties themselves. These theorists see parties as contributing to "justification," understood as legitimizing coercive laws within the contours of public reason, or to democratic deliberation. This literature stands as a correction to Disch's (2002, p. 108) observation that "today's proponents of deliberative and participatory democracy, schooled in the movement politics of the 1960's, hold party politics to be opportunistic, bureaucratic, and antithetical to citizenship."

Nonviolence, Regulated Rivalry, and Legitimate Opposition

The intellectual history of parties is largely a story of antipartyism and antipartisanship. For every effort to articulate a unified and stable order, parties and partisanship introduce political pluralism and with it division, dissension, and fragmentation. This is why, in its aim to describe a just and stable political order, political thought has been congenitally antipartisan.

Rosenblum (2008) identifies two historically recurrent forms of antipartyism, both still prominent today. In one, thinkers averse to social and political pluralism see parties as unwholesome parts; they disrupt some presumptive natural or aspirational unity, or holism. In the other, thinkers accept the fact of pluralism in politics (taking the form of corporatism or the mixed constitution, for example) but see political parties as dangerously divisive. The exception to historical antipartyism is the "last party," a party that is formed in response to an emergency and that disbands once the threat is allayed. But this—a party "to end all parties"—is the exception that proves the antiparty rule (Rosenblum 2008).

The guiding idea behind this defense of party is that if we accept pluralism, we cannot reject parties, and that the acceptance—indeed valuation—of pluralism entails political parties. There can never be one sole set of interests, or one authoritative interpretation of the common good. For that reason, rival positions should not be taken as purely strategic (Gutmann & Thompson 1996, p. 82). Transforming pluralism into ongoing, managed, institutionalized conflict among parties is a hard-won and fragile historical development (Hofstadter 1969). The legitimacy of the other side to compete for power is acknowledged. Rotation in office entails a method for determining winners and acceptance of the results by losers, including acceptance of policies they oppose. Crucially, opposition remains alive and continues; loss is not irreversible; "elections are not followed by waves of suicide" (Schattschneider 1942, p. 91). Regulated party rivalry for office distinguishes party opposition from sedition, treason, conspiracy, rebellion, or civil war.

The pluralist defense of parties is liberal insofar as it rejects political "holism" and any invocation of oneness—be it populism, fascism, theocracy, or a general will (Mouffe 2000, p. 21). It rejects any version of representation that rests on some ideal of totalism or unity, and it rejects every break with party politics motivated by abhorrence of division (Urbinati 2014, pp. 137, 144). It assigns to regulated party rivalry and loyal opposition the crucial business of making pluralism political by structuring conflict and legislative debate, shaping citizen choices, and holding the opposition accountable (Urbinati 2014, p. 229; Waldron 2016, p. 101).

Liberal too is the argument that regulated party rivalry normalizes and institutionalizes the "radical chastening" of political authority (Kateb 1992, p. 37). It undergirds the "provisional nature of political authority" (Rosenblum 2008, p. 363).

Political organization takes many forms, of course, but parties alone bring opposition into the frame of government (Fox & Nolte 1995, Waldron 2016). Waldron emphasizes that acceptance of party division as legitimate and acceptance of the loyal opposition are not adequately understood in terms of tolerance of disagreement, free speech and association, or even organized political opposition to government. A legitimate opposition is characterized by the principle of "positive empowerment" (Waldron 2016, p. 106): The opposition party has an officially recognized role within government—representation on legislative committees, for example (Waldron 2016, pp. 105–6; Rosenbluth & Shapiro 2018, pp. 36–38).

This political justification of parties raises the question of the bounds of loyal or legitimate opposition. How do we assess a charge that the opposition is not legitimate but rather is a conspiracy to undermine the nation or the constitution? If regulated party rivalry requires "a common grammar" (Urbinati 2019a, p. 102), how deep does that go?

The simplest criterion for banning or excluding party opposition is violence. This criterion would include party organizations that are fronts for paramilitary activity and insurrection. One difficulty is that evidence of complicity between armed militants and party leaders or members is always contested. And although violence excludes a party from the status of a loyal opposition, other extraelectoral actions do not—civil disobedience is not disqualifying, nor is using the electoral arena as a forum for mass political mobilization that then extends beyond campaigns and elections (Issacharoff 2015, p. 37).

A major strand of this literature on legitimate opposition addresses the question in terms of militant democracy: anticipatory measures taken by states to prohibit the formation or participation in elections of parties that exploit electoral politics to undermine democracy. The so-called paradox of democracy—restricting rights of political association if they threaten democracy—is not a paradox at all if we assume that "a Constitution is not a prescription for suicide" (Barak 2002, p. 44). The concept of militant democracy is the legacy of Weimar (Loewenstein 1937), but in practice, the standards and defensive measures written into law today closely track each nation's particular historical experiences (Rosenblum 2008, Kirschner 2014, Issacharoff 2015). Studies in this vein probe not only the bounds of legitimate opposition but also who polices these bounds—constitutional courts or legislatures or other entities (Issacharoff 2015, pp. 42 n.43, 60).

Within the rubric of militant democracy, then, standards vary. One measure of legitimate opposition on offer is adherence to established constitutional arrangements. Rawls (1993, pp. 227–30) makes the focus of loyalty "constitutional essentials," which include the idea of loyal opposition itself, arguing that frequent controversy over the structure of government undermines constitutional government. One difficulty here is defining "constitutional essentials." Another difficulty with adherence to constitutional arrangements as a standard of legitimate opposition is the propensity of parties to insert their positions into state or federal constitutions—prohibition of alcohol, for example, or bans on same-sex marriage—with the result that the constitution as currently interpreted cannot serve as the baseline of loyalty (Waldron 2016, p. 117).

Besides constitutional loyalty, a prominent justification for excluding or constraining parties is incitement of hatred toward a racial, ethnic, or religious subpopulation. Here, the concern is that party activity erodes democratic attitudes over the long term; for example, the aim of criminalizing neo-Nazi groups is not only to protect the state from Nazis but also to protect young people from Nazism. Another concern is that without constraint of parties, political hate speech intimidates voters and depresses participation.

Waldron shows the difficulty of isolating criteria for legitimate opposition, including adherence to electoral rules of the game or the amendment process. In place of a doctrinal or behavioral test, he proposes that loyal opposition refers to the way the opposition party must be regarded in a constitutional system. It works "as a sort of admonition to the ruling party" (Waldron 2016, p. 122). That is, the opposition is to be regarded as having constitutional and political standing to run the government (Waldron 2016, p. 120).

Whereas Rosenblum, Waldron, and Issacharoff argue that context and complexity militate against a single regulatory principle for defining, excluding, or limiting antidemocratic parties, Kirschner (2014, p. 25) provides one that applies to all political opposition, not parties specifically: "self-limiting" militant democracy. Antidemocrats have indefeasible rights to participate, on his view, and any exclusionary rule or ban should be limited to thwarting activities that violate others' core interests in participation.

The matter of legitimate opposition and measures to ban parties or otherwise constrain their activities is no longer restricted to antidemocratic parties or bound by the concept of militant democracy. Existential challenges have come to the fore. From this standpoint, political pluralism does not translate into legitimate opposition if parties use elections to transform the established idea of national identity (e.g., a Jewish state) or national political identity (e.g., secularism). However, the core idea behind the political justification of parties—the value of pluralism and its nonviolent institutionalization in regulated rivalry—argues that essentialist questions of identity too must be open to party contention (Rosenblum 2007, p. 67).

This political justification of parties (nonviolence, regulated rivalry, and legitimate opposition) has resonance today, when the fundamental value of pluralism and commitment to regulated rivalry—"that the losers of today may unseat the victors in a new round of electoral challenge"—is under attack, practically and ideologically (Issacharoff 2018, p. 485).

Public Reason

Theorists working within the framework of public reason defend parties in different terms. They value parties insofar as they take up the business of justifying the exercise of coercive authority in conformity with the requirements of public reason. Public reason is based on the elemental notion that to regard others as free and equal requires that the exercise of state power be justified with reasons open to the understanding of all and that others can accept. Philosophical accounts of public reason by Habermas (1995) and Rawls (1993, 1999) are frequent touchstones. This literature in defense of parties challenges the prevalent assumption that parties are identified with coercion, bargaining, and rhetorical manipulation and are fundamentally incompatible with public reason or, in a related defense discussed below, with deliberation (Christiano 1996).

Thus, Bonotti (2017) argues that Rawls' political liberalism nourishes parties by leaving many issues open to democratic contention. His "wide" concept of public reason allows the introduction of comprehensive doctrines in public discussion—provided that in due course public reasons are offered. On Bonotti's (2017, p. 123) interpretation, it falls to parties to identify those public reasons, and "an internal connection" exists between the demands of public reason and partisanship.

Working with a Habermasian conception of justification, White & Ypi (2016, p. 57), too, see "a deep structural affinity between the practices of partisanship and political justification." Partisanship is a politics of principle that speaks to the whole and is concerned to justify its commitments with general reasons. Moreover, insofar as justification is adversarial, party competition makes competing reasons accessible: It exposes citizens to political justification by demanding that reasons be engaged rather than censored, ignored, or dismissed.

For these theorists, parties are what make possible a politics of public reason. This is a view of parties from the outside; it revolves around an independent concept of justification and stands apart from existing political institutions. This work argues that parties can contribute to the circumstances of justification, but a lot is lost if parties are defensible only in these terms. To the extent that parties are valued mainly as agents of justification, other democratic purposes such as representation, political mobilization, and defining the terms of political division are eclipsed. To see parties in this way is to understate their role in linking government and pluralist civil society.

Muirhead & Rosenblum (2006, p. 99) take this up in their discussion of Rawls' express disdain for parties and "the great game of politics," which "betrays the marks of warfare." They argue that political liberalism nonetheless accommodates parties. Rawls admits that his view of the most reasonable conception of justice as fairness stands on a political spectrum and can be seen in partisan terms. Parties also unite what Rawls calls the background culture of society, where associations rooted in religious, moral, and philosophic ideas that do not comply with public reason have full play, and they bring the content of politics into the public political forum of constitutional democracy. Their value is not justification in terms of public reason but rather their "bilingual" translation between civil society and the constitutional sphere (Muirhead & Rosenblum 2006).

Parties and Deliberation

The thrust of deliberative democratic theory is its contrast to classic democratic theory's emphasis on voting in terms of pre-existing preferences that are "tainted by their causal history" (Beitz 1990, p. 179). Deliberation helps shape informed preferences and offers justifications of these preferences to others. Until recently, parties have been ignored or depreciated both as deliberating actors and as forums of deliberation. Instead, political theorists focus on designing special deliberative institutions: deliberative polls, citizen juries, and mini-publics. These are enhanced-information environments, with moderators guiding discussion, which yield decisions that are nonbinding, typically on a single issue. These deliberative settings are divorced from elections, and in some accounts partisans are explicitly excluded from participation. But there are exceptions. Hendriks et al. (2007, p. 362) ask, "Given that partisanship is an inevitable part of political life…how can it best be accommodated in deliberative practice?"

For many theorists, the goal of deliberation is arriving at impartial judgments of the common public interest, and the desired outcome is consensus. Yet not all theorists insist that deliberation reduces the scope or intensity of disagreement or aims at informed consensus or requires disinterestedness; clarifying aspects of commonality and disagreement is also a valued outcome (Gutmann & Thompson 2004). As accounts of democratic deliberation became more expansive, theorists began to consider not just specially designed deliberative settings but deliberative democracy writ large, in which parties have a role. Manin (1997, p. 15) proposes citizen deliberation informed by experts and moral authorities but allows participation by politicians provided it is decoupled from elections and campaigns. Parekh (2000, p. 306) prescribes public forums for cultivating "dialogically constituted multicultural society" and for making representations to the legislature, though he excludes parties in the legislature from serving this purpose. Ackerman & Fishkin (2004) prescribe "Deliberation Day"—nationwide citizen forums deliberating issues in anticipation of elections. They assign major parties a role in selecting issues and include debates between party representatives. That said, these deliberative settings are designed to stand outside of existing political institutions, and their decisions are not binding.

The agents of deliberation and its meaning and purpose are inseparable from institutional context, and normative theory lags behind empirical political science and positive political theory when it comes to the purpose of parties and party leadership in legislatures. There is little on the role of parties in areas such as agenda setting, committees, institutional rules and incentives, or the privileges of a minority party. Democratic theorists do consider whether and how partisan legislatures might function not only to publicize the reasons that ground these commitments, but also to prod "the parties to engage with the positions and the reasons of their adversaries in a way that informs citizens about the facts, the issues, and the options at hand" (Leydet 2015, p. 236; see also Mansbridge et al. 2012). Others question whether the party discipline that characterizes parliamentary government is consistent with the ethos of deliberation (Bhatia 2018). Work in this vein also challenges the sharp dichotomy that deliberative theorists sometime draw between political arguing and political bargaining (Habermas 1995, 1996; Elster 2000). Mansbridge et al. (2012) introduce the notion of "deliberative negotiation" based on mutual justification, respect, and reciprocal fairness, although the authors do not discuss partisan negotiation specifically. Finally, democratic theorists could do more work on the interbranch relations between parties and administrative agencies and courts (Schwartzberg & Knight 2020).

Hofstadter (1969, p. 72) emphasizes that deliberation "goes on not merely in the legislative process…but in the internal processes of the great political parties." Political theorists such as Wolkenstein and Invernizzi-Accetti attend to intraparty deliberation. Standard views see the internal working of candidate selection and agenda setting in terms of elites and already-formed preferences. In contrast, the argument for parties as deliberative forums emphasizes preference formation in local branches of the party. Intraparty deliberation from the bottom up connects the party base and government, on this view, so that parties mediate between society and the state (Wolkenstein 2016, Invernizzi-Accetti & Wolkenstein 2017). The argument is that parties' claims to be representative have declined because they have lost their deliberative and participatory qualities.

A broader argument about deliberation concerns parties in the open public sphere, engaged in shaping opinion and garnering support. At this level, parties do what philosophy cannot do, and what no other political organization can do as consistently or comprehensively: embrace and organize pluralism for democratic politics. Yet theorists of deliberative democracy have "abandoned mass democracy" (Chambers 2009, p. 323). Parties' creative political role has been given short shrift (Herman 2017, p. 741). Some theorists, however, have attended to the importance of parties for democratic deliberation in the wide sense. Rosenblum (2008) argues that they shape the range of matters for discussion and decision; parties create and articulate lines of division. Party rivalry focuses attention on specific problems, brings out information and interpretations, and delineates what is at stake. Without parties selecting and excluding, organizing and articulating issues, democratic theory's "trial by discussion" cannot be meaningful (Rosenblum 2008, p. 307). In institutional contexts like legislatures but also in the general public sphere, Muirhead (2019, p. 83) argues, "parties are necessary to deliberative democracy."

These normative defenses of parties argue that they can contribute to the circumstances of justification and to deliberation, but much of what makes parties defensible and valuable is left out. Some of what is left out, we have said, is fundamental to democracy: parties' organization of political pluralism and commitment to regulated rivalry and legitimate opposition. We now take up the question of parties' role in democratic citizenship and participation.

Citizenship, Partisanship, and Independence

Political participation is central to almost every conception of good democratic citizenship, but too little attention is paid to the critical connection between participation and representation as it is facilitated by parties (Urbinati & Warren 2008). In recent literature, parties are seen as essential for participation. A collective "we" is necessary to sustain and enhance political commitment, and parties keep the project visible and give it continuity over time. For Efthymiou (2018), for instance, partisanship is valuable because it supports political commitment and contestation. Parties inform, mobilize, and organize participation, and they connect government to citizens via "the partisan connection" (Muirhead & Rosenblum 2012). Their role includes education about political issues, "epistemic resiliency" to resist propaganda and misinformation (White & Ypi 2016, p. 93), and "cognitive mobilization" (Invernizzi-Accetti & Wolkenstein 2017, p. 98). Parties are a "useful training ground" for citizens to relate their comprehensive doctrines to liberal democracy, thus contributing to the overlapping consensus that guarantees stability (Bonotti 2017, p. 100). Another claim is that parties are "collective epistemic agents" that transform abstract value judgments into coherent conceptions of justice, reducing complexity, lowering the threshold of political competence, and creating epistemic equality (Ebeling 2016, pp. 650, 640). White & Ypi (2016, pp. 96, 210, 212–16) identify principles of party structure that enable a "democratic ethos." For Urbinati (2019b, p. 99), "[p]artisanship is in fact a term for thinking politically."

A stronger version asserts that to be a good citizen, one needs to be a partisan. Partisanship itself, not just partisanship as a spur to participation, is a civic ideal (White & Ypi 2016). What makes partisanship a defining element of good citizenship is that it enacts a commitment to pluralism: recognizing the legitimacy of opposition, complying with the rules of regulated rivalry, and accepting the partiality of partisan claims. The "moral distinctiveness" of partisanship lies in "commitment to the provisional nature of political authority, its periodic recreation" (Kateb 1981, p. 358). The usual view is that, to serve their valuable purposes, parties require partisans, but it is also the case that parties are necessary to realize the value of partisanship (Rosenblum 2008, p. 367).

Today, the normative value of partisanship is challenged by claims that Independents have superior moral standing. In this view, parties may be a systemic sine qua non of democracy, but partisan citizens are not. Rather, democracy requires free-thinking, independent-minded citizens and representatives who are not swayed by party loyalty, who weigh rival claims, and who go where the facts and evidence lead them. The logic of this view is that Independent status is not adequately characterized as nonpartisanship but, in the United States at least, as a distinct political identity that entails antipartisanship (Rosenblum 2008).

Independents are defined in contrast to partisans, who are said to be bought, or vulnerable to the undue influence of activists, or who are themselves extremists who contribute to the skewing of representation and the polarization of politics. The claim is that Independents constitute a more deliberative public and arrive at an unbiased estimate of the public good (Dalton et al. 2000, p. 60). The normative ideal of independence has institutional consequences, among them nonpartisan primary elections that reflect antiparty animus and whose constitutionality has been the subject of US Supreme Court cases (Thompson 2002).

Standing for principles has integrity; this is what the normative ideal of independence is about. But for defenders of partisanship, antipartisan voters are "not self-reliant but weightless" (Wolfe 2000, p. 15). Politics is not only about standing for. It is always also about standing with. This—standing with others—is the challenge of the ethics of partisanship.

The Ethics of Partisanship

The ethics of partisanship has two aspects. From one standpoint, it consists of constraints on the partisan's pursuit of actions that might be tempting or effective, but are wrong judged by standards external to partisanship. For instance, White & Ypi (2016, p. 2) emphasize that standards of political justification should constrain partisanship. The second aspect of the ethics of partisanship denotes virtues distinctive to partisans that are cultivated and expressed through partisan activity. The most fundamental of these is the willingness to stand with others in a group sufficiently capacious that it can act with democratic legitimacy (Muirhead 2006, White & Ypi 2016). Within this framework, we find the characteristics that political theorists most often identify with ethical partisanship: inclusivity, comprehensiveness, compromise, and loyalty.

Inclusivity is the desire to win office (and power) on the most democratic terms possible—with a popular mandate. As an empirical matter, some might see the inclination to inclusivity as solely the result of electoral incentives established by the electoral rules of the game, and the necessity to build a large electoral coalition will depend on whether a system is first past the post or proportional. Inclusivity implies that parties in democracies will not pursue disenfranchisement because such antidemocratic strategies will never be in their interest. When Schattschneider (1942, p. 1) wrote that "political parties created democracy," he tacitly invoked this idea that democratization works in only one direction—the franchise is extended but not retracted. But retractions of the franchise do occur. Some parties make democracy, as Schattschneider said; others can diminish it—or destroy it (L. E. Herman & R. Muirhead, unpublished manuscript). With respect to inclusivity, electoral incentives matter enormously, yet are insufficient. Partisans also need an ethical commitment to inclusivity, understood as winning on democratic terms.

Comprehensiveness is what definitionally separates a party from a faction, or what Sartori (1976, p. 25) calls "only a part for itself" (Bonotti 2017, p. 10). Comprehensiveness means that partisans take a view on the full range of issues that constitute the public interest—from the economy to national security. In contrast to single-issue advocacy groups, parties address the public good in the widest sense. This is why parties have platforms that do not claim to benefit just one group at the expense of others, but to benefit the nation. At their best, partisans attempt to address the common good, even though they do not presume to speak for the whole. In White & Ypi's (2016, p. 53) terms, partisans should be "nonpartial."

One might argue that comprehensiveness is more evident in large coalitions, but there is no correlation between the raw size of a party and the comprehensiveness of its arguments and platform. Small parties and parties of conscientious dissent might address questions of justice and the national interest more comprehensively—and, for many, more compellingly—than the large parties that dominate a party system.

Inclusivity and comprehensiveness lead to the third element of ethical partisanship, a disposition to seek compromise. For some thinkers, compromise is the signal virtue of parties. This was the view, for instance, of Hans Kelsen, whose 1929 *On the Essence and Value of Democracy* justified parties mainly in terms of their role in "creating the organizational conditions" for compromise and "moving the common will toward a median" [Kelsen 2013 (1929), quoted by Mersel (2006), p. 163]. Kelsen's arguments and his theory of "party democracy" command the attention of a new generation of democratic theorists working on partisanship (Ragazzoni 2017). While the possibility that parties might compromise with each other was central to Kelsen's thought, it is important to recall that the disposition to compromise is located within parties as well: Without an ability to compromise with copartisans, there is no party, no group large enough to legitimately govern.

The Spirit of Compromise by Gutmann & Thompson (2012) is a comprehensive discussion of the political need for a "compromising mindset" and the inseparability of the question from institutional context. The authors distinguish compromise, which entails mutual sacrifice and likely internal incoherence in the result, from "common ground." They reject the interest/principle distinction as a way of evaluating political compromise. Adapting one's principles ("principled prudence") and respecting the opposition are set against standing on principle and against the mistrust of opponents that characterize the uncompromising mindset. Rosenblum (2008, p. 42), too, argues in this vein: Uncompromisingness inhibits the public business from getting done, and therefore represents an abdication of responsibility for governing.

Consistent with this, Beerbohm (2018) locates compromise as a democratic practice peculiar to the legislator's role. He argues from the vantage point of what he calls "co-ownership." Compromise is defensible insofar as concessions "honor the procedural value of deciding together." Compromise "can raise a law's democratic credentials," and it can increase the "force of bipartisanship in a two-party system" (Beerbohm 2018, pp. 6, 30).

Whether compromise is part of the ethics of partisanship is disputed. Some think that the epistemic significance of political disagreement argues for "conciliation" rather than "compromise and consensus" (Ebeling 2016). White & Ypi (2016, pp. 142–63), too, challenge the importance of compromise. Although they concede that particular compromises may be advisable, "as an ideal, political justification constrained by norms of public reason is always to be preferred over the politics of compromise" (White & Ypi 2016, p. 163). A different standard connects the limits of compromise "to the life of the partisan project itself"; to compromise too much is to risk losing the soul of the party (Urbinati 2019b, p. 100).

The counterpoint to compromise is loyalty—the quintessential partisan virtue, without which any standing with others is impossible. Loyalty has its hazards: It can render one blind to all facts and events that seem bad for one's party and one's cause. But accomplishing anything ambitious in politics requires loyalty because policies and programs take time to be worked out, and those opposed to the policy or program will not relax their opposition while things unfold. Loyal partisans are patient in their support for their candidates, their plans, and their programs (Muirhead 2013).

Bonotti (2017, pp. 16–17), by contrast, argues that partisans should not be loyal to their party. They should rather think of themselves as having obligations to civility and fair play to other partisans, even rival partisans. The ethical obligations of fair play are stringent side constraints on the partisan pursuit of power—not least constraining what they can do out of loyalty to their own party.

Both with respect to the ethics of partisanship (e.g., the quality of inclusiveness) and the side constraints that restrict what partisans qua partisans should do in order to win, partisanship entails a commitment to constitutional democracy. In particular, it entails a commitment to pluralism, to parties as a vital institutionalization of pluralism, and to the idea of legitimate opposition. Without this commitment, the ethics of partisanship dissolve. Not even the best constitutional design or electoral system can create an incentive structure that reliably motivates partisans to act in ways that sustain democracy even as they seek to advance themselves.

Conclusion: The Delegitimation of Parties and Partisanship, Again

Political theorists have come to parties and partisanship late in the day. The qualities that enlisted parties and partisans in the project of making democracy (Schattschneider 1942) may be disappearing; certainly representative democracy is under more stress than at any time since the 1930s. Understanding and navigating the challenges and threats of the moment requires political theory that engages political science—and vice versa (Van Biezen & Saward 2008, Herman 2017).

Two specific considerations are needed in theorists' thinking about parties today. One is attention to new forces permeating the public sphere and undermining deliberation in the broadest sense—including the regulated rivalry of political parties. In addition to the usual menu of obstructions (self-interest, insufficient information, partisan bias, the distortion of dark money, and more), the forces of conspiracism and disinformation have taken center stage. They are creating an epistemic chasm among citizens as significant as partisan polarization, making it impossible not only to compromise and negotiate, but even to disagree (Muirhead & Rosenblum 2019). What is at stake is the norm of a legitimate opposition. The practices associated with this norm are always delicate, if only because the idea itself is so subtle. How can we view an opponent whose program we take to be mistaken, even catastrophically so, as also legitimate? The answer depends less on manners of respect than on the rituals and actions that signal loyalty to rules of fair competition and to the democratic constitution itself. But if epistemic polarization makes opponents impossible to understand and impossible not to perceive as a threat, rituals like concession speeches after an election loss will not be sufficient to fortify the norm.

The second, even more disturbing consideration is that the incentives to ethical partisanship—inclusiveness, comprehensiveness, and the disposition to compromise—are under stress, and in the absence of ethical partisans, they may be insufficient to sustain these qualities in the future. Partisans today often give up on inclusivity and pursue strategies that depend on disenfranchising opposition voters. Rather than offer a comprehensive account of the common good, they settle for activating their base. Instead of building a legislative coalition through compromise, they impede and obstruct "on principle," seeming to prefer symbolic stands to governing.

Partisans at their best avoid claiming the kind of legitimacy that comes from representing the people as a whole. At the same time, they strive to rule with democratic legitimacy by forging a large and lasting coalition. Is modern society so fragmented that the partisan quest to build a lasting (but never permanent) majority or coalition is out of reach? Or is it rather that the political virtues of coalition-building—inclusivity and comprehensiveness—have been displaced by the moral virtues of independence or uncompromising integrity, giving rise to a politics of self-righteous postures? In the future as in the past, the challenge of making democracy work will fall to partisans who take on the task of making parties work.

Over the past 15 years, political theorists have identified and defended the normative terms of parties and partisanship. This has improved democratic theory. Our concern is whether these defenses can also improve our capacity to counter new forms of antipartyism that buffet democratic institutions.

When Deliberative Agreement Isn't Possible, Political Parties Provide Structure for Democratic Governance

Ian Shapiro

Ian Shapiro is professor of political science at Yale University and previously served as the Henry R. Luce Director of the MacMillan Center for International and Area Studies at Yale from 2004 to 2019. He is a fellow of the American Academy of Arts and Sciences and the American Philosophical Society, as well as a member of the Council on Foreign Relations.

Advocates of political deliberation usually defend it as a collaborative activity motivated by the possibility of agreement. Even when agreement proves elusive, deliberation helps people come to grips with one another's views, draw on their different experiences and expertise, and better understand the contours of their enduring disagreements. People's views will be better informed, and the decisions they make will be of higher quality than if they had not deliberated. When study after study reveals most people to be appallingly ill-informed about much public policy, deliberation's appeal seems obvious. Two minds are better than one, three better than two, and so on. Democracy will be improved if its decision-making can incorporate, and build on, the benefits of deliberation. Or so it is frequently claimed.[1]

Deliberation should not be confused with argument. When people argue, there is an expectation that one of them will, or at least should, win. Even when we speak of one person making an argument, we see this as something that stands until it is contradicted, or challenged and beaten by a better argument. Like the deliberationists, proponents of argument believe it will enhance understanding and improve the quality of decisions. This was the

"Collusion in Restraint of Democracy: Against Political Deliberation," by Ian Shapiro, Copyright © 2017 by Ian Shapiro. Reprinted by permission.

essence of John Stuart Mill's defense of the robust clash of opinions in *On Liberty*: it would lead people to hold better-informed and more accurate views. Mill even went so far as to worry—needlessly, it turned out—that as advancing science expanded the realm of settled knowledge, people would be deprived of argument's benefits. No longer forced to sharpen their wits by defending their views in the marketplace of ideas, they would become mediocre dullards; less able to think for themselves and more easily manipulated by others.[2]

My claim here is that the argumentative and deliberative ideals should be more clearly distinguished than they usually are. They support different and incompatible institutional arrangements. I also maintain that the argumentative ideal is superior because, when appropriately institutionalized, it helps hold governments accountable for their actions. By contrast, the deliberative ideal cannot easily be institutionalized—and perhaps cannot be institutionalized at all—because people who prefer to bargain can easily abuse rules designed to promote deliberation. But deliberation's difficulties run deeper. Its defenders fail to appreciate that, in politics, deliberation and the search for agreement are— to borrow an antitrust analogy—unhealthy forms of collusion in restraint of democracy. They should worry less about voter ignorance, which, as Anthony Downs noted long ago, might well reflect sensible budgeting of scarce time, and worry more when office-seekers fail to engage in robust public debates over the policies that, if elected, they will enact.[3]

Joseph Schumpeter's competitive model of democracy, in which governments acquire power by prevailing in a "competitive struggle for the people's vote," gives institutional expression to the argumentative ideal.[4] This was perhaps best exemplified in the Westminster system as it existed from 1911, when the Parliament Act stripped the House of Lords of its real powers, until the late 1990s, when the Lords was reformed to enhance its legitimacy as a second chamber and the Commons began ceding authority to European and other courts, the Bank of England, and independent agencies. The twentieth century's middle eight decades were the heyday of Parliament's supremacy within the British political system and of the Commons' supremacy within Parliament. Epitomized at Prime Minister's Questions, the sometimes overwrought weekly gladiatorial clashes over the famous wooden despatch boxes, it thrives on the ongoing contest between opposing policies and ideologies.

Schumpeterian democracy depends on alternation between two strong parties in government. The party that wins the election exercises a temporary power monopoly, but the loyal opposition—a government-in-waiting whose leaders hope to take power at the next election—continually challenges its policies. This system depends on combining first-past-the-post single member plurality (SMP) electoral systems with parliamentary democracy. The SMP electoral system produces two large parties, so long as the political makeup of the constituencies more or less reflects the political makeup of the national population.[5] Parliamentary systems ensure that the parties will be strong because the leader of the majority party is also the chief executive. Government and opposition clash across the aisle continually, and compete during elections by offering voters the different programs they plan to implement.

The deliberative model, by contrast, calls for institutions that create incentives to seek agreement rather than victory—or at least agreement as a condition for victory. Rules that require concurrent majorities in bicameral chambers force representatives to find common ground when they can, and compromise when they cannot. Executive vetoes and supermajority provisions to override them create similar incentives. Proponents of deliberation often find proportional representation (PR) congenial for comparable reasons. Instead of two catchall parties that must submerge their disagreements in order to win elections, PR leads to party proliferation, bringing a more diverse array of voices to the political table. In addition to the left-of-center and right-of-center parties characteristic of SMP systems, in PR systems, liberals, religious groups, Greens, separatists, and nationalists, among others, can all elect representatives to the legislature to be part of the conversation. Because one party seldom wins an absolute majority, coalition government, which forces parties to seek and perhaps even manufacture common ground, is the norm.

The US system is a hybrid. The SMP electoral system produces two large parties, but the independently elected president weakens them, and the system of checks and balances forces consensus-seeking and compromise to the extent possible. The American founders intended the Senate, in particular, to be a constraining body made up of what Jefferson would later refer to as an "aristocracy of virtue and talent." It has been heralded as such by commentators dating back at least to Alexis de Tocqueville.[6] The idea that the Senate is the world's greatest deliberative body, which first gained currency with Daniel Webster's three-hour soliloquy in defense of the Union in 1850, has been repeated to the point of banality, no matter how scant its connection with reality.[7] I will have more to say about the kind of competition the US system fosters shortly. As a prelude to this, notice that, unlike the Westminster model, which gives temporary control of the government's power monopoly to the majority party and relies on alternation over time as its main mechanism of accountability, the US model divides up the control of power on an ongoing basis. Madison's slogan was that "ambition must be made to counteract ambition."[8] The checks and balances force the players in the different branches to accommodate themselves to one another; hence its affinities with the deliberative ideal.

Up to a point. A major limitation of institutions that encourage deliberation is that they can produce bargaining instead. Juries, for example, are traditionally subject to unanimity requirements that put pressure on their members to talk out their differences until they reach agreement. When this works well, it produces thorough exploration of all the arguments and evidence provided by the contending parties: a poster child for the benefits of deliberation. But a jury can also be held hostage by a recalcitrant crank who has nothing better to do when everyone else wants to go home.

His superior bargaining power and stubbornness might enable him to extract agreement from the others, but this will not be deliberative consensus on the merits of the case. What holds for juries also holds for other institutions that we might hope will induce deliberation. When they produce bargaining instead, those with the most leverage will prevail. So it is that small parties often exert disproportionate influence over coalition governments, US Senators can use holds and filibuster rules to thwart the will of the majority, and various other super majority and concurrent majority rules can be deployed to similar effect.

In short, deliberation requires people to act in good faith, but it is not possible to design institutions to induce good faith. "If men were angels," Madison wrote, "no government would be necessary."[9] Indeed, when power is at stake and representatives must answer to constituents, the impulse to bargain will likely overpower even genuine desires to reason collaboratively. In 2009, a number of centrist Republican Senators showed an interest in working with the Obama White House for "cap-and-trade" legislation on toxic emissions control. They soon bolted, however, when confronted with Tea Party–orchestrated threats of primary challenges in their constituencies, should they choose to persist.[10] Since power is endemically at stake in politics, it seems unlikely that there will be much genuine deliberation or that politicians will resist the impulse to exploit rules that might maximize their leverage instead.

An exception that proves the rule is the British House of Lords. It functioned most effectively as a deliberative body after it lost most of its real powers in 1911. Peers who participated were mainly public-spirited individuals who specialized in particular areas and were often nonpartisan or crossbenchers. But the Lords has become more partisan and assertive since the 1999 reforms restored a measure of its legitimacy as a somewhat democratic institution, albeit one at a considerable distance from the ballot box.[11] What the Lords has gained in legitimacy has come at the price of diminished effectiveness as a deliberative institution.[12]

The various deliberative institutions that have been tried out or proposed in recent years are exclusively consultative. Deliberative Polls and citizens' juries have no authority to decide anything. They might affect how people vote, but it is the voting that will be decisive. Objects of theoretical conjecture like ideal speech situations are even more radically divorced from politics, since they depend on armchair speculation about what people would decide in settings that are devoid of power relationships. Questions can and have been raised about whether such speculations add up to anything we should believe, or whether the changes in people's views produced by Deliberative Polls and other consultative mechanisms tried thus far are really improvements on their pre-deliberative views or simply changes.[13] These issues need not detain us here, however, since my present point is that—whatever its merits—institutionalizing deliberation turns out to be an elusive endeavor. If it is purely consultative, it is not clear why anyone will or should pay attention to it. Yet if rules are created to institutionalize deliberation and give it real decision-making teeth, they can all too easily undermine political competition and empower people with leverage to appropriate them for their own purposes.

Schumpeter's competitive model of democracy trades on analogies between the political marketplace of ideas and the economy. Political parties are the analogues of firms; voters mirror consumers. Schumpeter treats the policies that parties propose to enact if they become governments as the political analogues of the goods and services that firms sell, and the votes that politicians seek as analogues of the revenues that firms try to earn. Democratic accountability is the political equivalent of consumer sovereignty: the party that does best at satisfying voters wins their support.

Schumpeter's illuminating analogy is nonetheless strained in several ways, two of which matter here. One is that political parties are vying to control a monopoly, a fact that constrains competitive possibilities. As I argue below, the best option is competition between two large, centrally controlled parties. The Schumpeterian analogy also falters because there is no unproblematic equivalent of a firm's shareholders for political parties. Some will single out party members or activists as the appropriate political shareholders, but parties that empower them run into trouble. Membership in political parties is typically free or very cheap, rendering them susceptible to hostile and anomalous takeovers, like that perpetrated by Donald Trump in the 2016 Republican primaries, or that which occurred in the British Labour Party in the summer of 2016. Party leader Jeremy Corbyn lost a confidence vote in the Parliamentary Labour Party by 172 to 40 in June, triggering a leadership challenge, but an easily augmented membership nonetheless reelected him as leader with 61.8 percent of the vote three months later.[14] As this example underscores, grass roots activists tend to be unrepresentative of a party's supporters in the electorate. This imbalance can be especially pronounced in two-party systems, which, as I argue below, are nonetheless best from the standpoint of robust public debate.

Representation should be geared to maximizing the chances that public debate will center on the policies that parties, if elected, will implement as governments.[15] This is why SMP beats PR, and why strong, centralized parties are better than weak, decentralized ones. Supporting a party in a multiparty system can help voters feel better represented because their representatives' views are likely closer to their ideals than would be the case in a two-party system. But this is an illusion. What really matters is the policies that governments will implement. That cannot be known until after the coalition is formed, post-election. Coalition governments decrease accountability, since different coalition members can blame one another for unpopular policies.[16] Americans got a taste of this when unusual conditions produced a cross-party coalition to enact the Budget Sequestration Act in August 2011, putting in place $1.1 trillion of automatic spending cuts over eight years split evenly between defense and domestic programs, unless Congress passed an alternative by January 2013. The Sword-of-Damocles proposal was widely said to be sufficiently draconian that the representatives would be forced to find a compromise. In the event, they did not and the sword fell, with each side blaming the other for intransigence. Perhaps it was a cynical way for both parties to achieve cuts without being savaged by their electoral bases. Whether due to blundering or collusive cynicism, the result was that everyone had an alibi and no one was undeniably responsible for the outcome. Coalition governments live perpetually on such ambiguous terrain, undermining accountability for what governments actually do.

Competition enhances political accountability, but some kinds of competition are better than others. As we have seen, competition between representatives of two parties, one of which will become the government, enhances accountability because they run on the platform they will be judged on as governments. Moreover, the need to sustain broad bases of voter support gives them strong incentives to advocate policies that will be good for the country as a whole, or at least for large swaths of the population. Smaller parties represent more narrowly drawn interests: business, organized labor, and ethnic and religious groups. This loads the dice in favor of clientelism, because politicians know that they will be held accountable for how effectively they advocate or bargain for their group's interests in a governing coalition. It is better for parties to compete over what is best for the country as a whole than to bargain over the rents they can extract for their clients. This contrast can be overdrawn, to be sure, because large catchall parties consist of different interests among whom implicit bargains must be struck to keep them in the party. But that bargaining is constrained by the need to propound and defend platforms that can win support from other groups as well, otherwise they cannot hope to become the government.

The sequester episode underscores the fact that the weakness of US political parties is only partly due to republican institutional arrangements. Another source of party weakness is decentralized competition, an artifact of the wrongheaded idea that local selection of candidates somehow makes the process more democratic. In reality, because of their comparatively high rates of participation, activists, whose beliefs and preferences tend to be both more extreme and more intensely held than the median voter in their constituencies, dominate primaries and caucuses. This enables them to force representatives to pursue agendas that the median voter in their district abjures, or to serve the median voter only with the kind of subterfuge that might have been at work behind the Budget Sequester Act. The same is true of referenda, which sound democratic—"hooray for direct democracy!"—but which also enfranchise intense single-issue voters who turn out at disproportionately high rates. Thus it was with the Brexit referendum in June of 2016, when a majority of those who voted produced the result to leave, even though polling indicated that the median British voter favored the UK's remaining in the European Union, as did substantial majorities of both major parties in the House of Commons.[17]

Some will say that making the system responsive to voters with intense preferences is a good thing. There is, indeed, a strand of democratic theory dating back to James Buchannan and Gordon Tullock's *Calculus of Consent* in 1962 whose proponents defend vote trading and vote buying on the utilitarian ground that it improves the overall social utility.[18] But democracy's purpose is to manage power relations, not to maximize social utility. The contrary view would suggest that it was right for the US government to abandon Reconstruction when Southern whites opposed it with greater intensity than most voters favored it, and that it was right for the intense preferences of neoconservatives who wanted the United States to invade Iraq in 2003 to override those of more numerous but less-fervent skeptics.[19] This is to say nothing of the fact that in politics, preferences are always expressed subject to budget constraints. The intense antiregulation preferences of the multibillionaires Charles and David Koch are massively amplified because their budget constraints differ vastly from those of the typical voter.[20] In short, there are good reasons for the rules of democratic decision-making to reflect how many people want something, rather than how intensely they want it.

People have theorized about democracy for millennia, yet it is only in the past few decades that the idea has gained currency that democracy depends on, or at any rate can be substantially enhanced by, deliberation. I have sought to show here that this is a dubious proposition. It is hard, if not impossible, to create institutions that will foster deliberation in politics, and institutions designed to do so are all-too-easily hijacked for other purposes. But deliberation is in any case the wrong goal. Competition is the lifeblood of democratic politics, and not just because it is the mechanism by which governments that lose elections give up power. Institutions that foster competition also structure politics around argument, which Mill was right to identify as vital to the advancement of knowledge and good public policy.

But not any competition. The contestation over governing ideas that Mill prized is best served when two large parties are constrained to compete over potential governing programs. It is compromised by multiparty competition that encourages clientelism, as we have seen. And it is damaged even more by competition within parties, which empowers people with local agendas and intense preferences who participate disproportionately in primaries and caucuses. This can render parties vulnerable to the ideological capture of candidates by well-funded groups, as has happened with the Tea Party in Southern and Midwestern Republican primaries since 2009. But a more general problem is associated with local control of selection processes, in which candidates find themselves compelled to compete by promising to secure local goods. Once elected, they face powerful incentives to engage in pork barrel politics with other similarly situated politicians, protecting public funding for sinecures and bridges to nowhere in their districts. This problem is worse in districts—the vast majority in the United States—that have been gerrymandered to be safe seats, so that the primary is the only meaningful election. It is better for party leaders to seek candidates who can both win in their districts and support a program that can win nationally. The leaders, in turn, are held accountable by the backbenchers who remove them when they fail to deliver winning platforms. In sum, two large, centrally controlled parties are most likely to foster the programmatic competition that is best for democratic politics. By contrast, multi-party competition encourages wholesale clientelism, and intraparty competition encourages retail clientelism.

Deliberation can be rendered harmless and perhaps, occasionally, beneficial for democratic politics by relegating it to a purely consultative role; but in that case, it is hard to see what the hype surrounding deliberation amounts to. Regardless, the most pressing political challenges in the United States do not result from lack of deliberation. Rather, they stem from the increasing subversion of democracy by powerful private interests since the Supreme Court's disastrous equation of money with speech in *Buckley v. Valeo* four decades ago, and the subsequent playing out of that logic in *Citizens United* and subsequent decisions.[21] As politicians have become increasingly dependent on countless millions of dollars to gain and retain political office, those with the resources they need undermine the process by manufacturing—and then manning—huge barriers to entry, by contributing to both political parties in ways that stifle competition, by capturing regulators and whole regulatory agencies, by giving multimillionaires and billionaires the preposterous advantage of running self-funded campaigns, and by doing other end-runs around democratic politics. Unless and until that challenge can be addressed, debating what deliberation can add to politics is little more than a waste of time.

Endnotes

1. For example, see Jane J. Mansbridge, *Beyond Adversary Democracy*, 2nd ed. (Chicago: University of Chicago Press, 1983); Amy Gutmann and Dennis Thompson, *Democracy and Disagreement* (Cambridge, Mass.: Harvard University Press, 1996); Amy Gutmann and Dennis Thompson, *Why Deliberative Democracy* (Princeton, N.J.: Princeton University Press, 2009); James S. Fishkin, *The Voice of the People* (New Haven, Conn.: Yale University Press, 1995); James S. Fishkin, *When the People Speak: Deliberative Democracy and Public Consultation* (Oxford: Oxford University Press, 2011); Hélène Landemore, *Democratic Reason: Politics, Collective Intelligence, and the Rule of the Many* (Princeton, N.J.: Princeton University Press, 2012); Jürgen

Habermas, *Communication and the Evolution of Society* (Boston: Beacon Press, 1975); and Jürgen Habermas, *The Theory of Communicative Action* (Boston: Beacon Press, 1984). There are, of course, major differences among these and other theorists of deliberative democracy that do not concern me here.

2. John Stuart Mill, *On Liberty*, ed. David Bromwich (New Haven, Conn.: Yale University Press, 2003 [1859]), 86–120.

3. See Anthony Downs, *An Economic Theory of Democracy* (New York: Harper and Row, 1957), 244–246, 266–271.

4. Joseph Schumpeter, *Capitalism, Socialism, and Democracy* (London: George Allen & Unwin, 1942), 269.

5. Where there is substantial regional variation, by contrast, as in India, SMP systems can produce party proliferation.

6. Tocqueville described the Senate as peopled by America's "ablest citizens"; men moved by "lofty thoughts and generous instincts." By contrast, the House of Representatives consisted of "village lawyers, tradesmen, or even men of the lowest class" who were of "vulgar demeanor," animated by "vices" and "petty passions." Alexis de Tocqueville, *Democracy in America*, ed. J. P. Mayer (New York: Anchor Books, 1969 [1835, 1840]), 200–201.

7. Terence Samuel, *The Upper House: A Journey behind Closed Doors* (New York: Palgrave MacMillan, 2010), 68.

8. James Madison, "Federalist No. 51," in *The Federalist Papers*, ed. Ian Shapiro (New Haven, Conn.: Yale University Press, 2009 [1787–1788]), 264.

9. Ibid.

10 Jane Mayer, *Dark Money: The Hidden History of the Billionaires behind the Rise of the Radical Right* (New York: Doubleday, 2016), 198–225.

11. The House of Lords Act of 1999 reduced the membership from 1,330 to 699 and got rid of all but ninety-two of the hereditary peers, who were allowed to remain on an interim basis, and an additional ten who were made life peers. On the recent evolution, see Meg Russell, *The Contemporary House of Lords: Westminster Bicameralism Revived* (Oxford: Oxford University Press, 2013), 13–35, 258–284.

12. For elaboration, see Ian Shapiro, *Politics against Domination* (Cambridge, Mass.: Harvard University Press, 2016), 73–78.

13. See Ian Shapiro, *The Real World of Democratic Theory* (Princeton, N.J.: Princeton University Press, 2010), 266–271.

14. James Lyons and Sanya Burgess, "Corbyn Reelected as Labour Leader with Increased Mandate," *The Times*, September 24, 2016, http://www.thetimes.co.uk/edition/news/corbyn-re-elected-as-labour-leader-with-increased-mandate-c7jqjgjm7.

15. The argument in this and the next two paragraphs will be developed more fully in Frances Rosenbluth and Ian Shapiro, *Democratic Competition: The Good,*

the Bad, and the Ugly (New Haven, Conn.: Yale University Press, forthcoming 2018).

16. Kathleen Bawn and Frances Rosenbluth, "Short versus Long Coalitions: Electoral Accountability and the Size of the Public Sector," *American Journal of Political Science* 50 (2) (2006): 251–265.

17. Charlie Cooper, "EU Referendum: Final Polls Show Remain with Edge over Brexit," *The Independent*, June 23, 2016, http://www.independent.co.uk/news /uk/politics/eu-referendum-poll-brexit-remain-vote-leave-live-latest-who-will -win-results-populus-a7097261.html; and Anushka Asthana, "Parliamentary Fightback against Brexit on Cards," *The Guardian*, June 26, 2016, http://www .theguardian.com/politics/2016/jun/26/fightback-against-brexit-on-cards -remain-eu-referendum-heseltine.

18. James Buchanan and Gordon Tullock, *The Calculus of Consent: Logical Foundations of Constitutional Democracy* (Ann Arbor: University of Michigan Press, 1962). Robert Dahl flirted with the notion that attending to intensity might be desirable from the standpoint of political stability, though he was skeptical that it could be measured. Robert Dahl, *A Preface to Democratic Theory* (Chicago: University of Chicago Press, 1956), 90–123.

19. For discussion of the dangers inherent in catering to intense preferences, see Shapiro, *Politics against Domination*, 46–61.

20. See Mayer, *Dark Money*, 120–158, 226–270, 354–387.

21. See *Buckley v. Valeo* 424 US 1, 59 (1976); *Citizens United v. Federal Election Commission* 558 US 310 (2010); and *SpeechNow.org v. Federal Election Commission* 599 F.3d 686, 689 (D.C. Cir. 2010).

Democracies Fail from Within

Steven Levitsky and Daniel Ziblatt

Steven Levitsky is professor of government and director of the David Rockefeller Center for Latin American Studies at Harvard University. He is the author of several books on democracy, authoritarianism, and political institutions. Daniel Ziblatt is professor of the science of government at Harvard University and co-chair of the Seminar on Democracy: Past, Future, and Present at the Minda de Gunzburg Center for European Studies.

B latant dictatorship—in the form of fascism, communism, or military rule—has disappeared across much of the world. Military coups and other violent seizures of power are rare. Most countries hold regular elections. Democracies still die, but by different means.

Since the end of the Cold War, most democratic breakdowns have been caused not by generals and soldiers but by elected governments themselves. Like Hugo Chávez in Venezuela, elected leaders have subverted democratic institutions in Georgia, Hungary, Nicaragua, Peru, the Philippines, Poland, Russia, Sri Lanka, Turkey and Ukraine.

Democratic backsliding today begins at the ballot box. The electoral road to breakdown is dangerously deceptive. With a classic coup d'état, as in Pinochet's Chile, the death of a democracy is immediate and evident to all. The presidential palace burns. The president is killed, imprisoned or shipped off into exile. The constitution is suspended or scrapped.

On the electoral road, none of these things happen. There are no tanks in the streets. Constitutions and other nominally democratic institutions remain in place. People still vote. Elected autocrats maintain a veneer of democracy while eviscerating its substance.

"How Democracies Die," by Steven Levitsky and Daniel Ziblatt, Guardian News and Media Limited, January 21, 2018, Reprinted by permission.

Many government efforts to subvert democracy are "legal," in the sense that they are approved by the legislature or accepted by the courts. They may even be portrayed as efforts to improve democracy—making the judiciary more efficient, combating corruption or cleaning up the electoral process.

Newspapers still publish but are bought off or bullied into self-censorship. Citizens continue to criticize the government but often find themselves facing tax or other legal troubles. This sows public confusion. People do not immediately realize what is happening. Many continue to believe they are living under a democracy.

Because there is no single moment—no coup, declaration of martial law, or suspension of the constitution—in which the regime obviously "crosses the line" into dictatorship, nothing may set off society's alarm bells. Those who denounce government abuse may be dismissed as exaggerating or crying wolf. Democracy's erosion is, for many, almost imperceptible.

How vulnerable is American democracy to this form of backsliding? The foundations of our democracy are certainly stronger than those in Venezuela, Turkey or Hungary. But are they strong enough?

Answering such a question requires stepping back from daily headlines and breaking news alerts to widen our view, drawing lessons from the experiences of other democracies around the world and throughout history.

A comparative approach reveals how elected autocrats in different parts of the world employ remarkably similar strategies to subvert democratic institutions. As these patterns become visible, the steps toward breakdown grow less ambiguous—and easier to combat. Knowing how citizens in other democracies have successfully resisted elected autocrats, or why they tragically failed to do so, is essential to those seeking to defend American democracy today.

We know that extremist demagogues emerge from time to time in all societies, even in healthy democracies. The United States has had its share of them, including Henry Ford, Huey Long, Joseph McCarthy and George Wallace.

An essential test for democracies is not whether such figures emerge but whether political leaders, and especially political parties, work to prevent them from gaining power in the first place—by keeping them off mainstream party tickets, refusing to endorse or align with them and, when necessary, making common cause with rivals in support of democratic candidates.

Isolating popular extremists requires political courage. But when fear, opportunism or miscalculation leads established parties to bring extremists into the mainstream, democracy is imperiled.

Once a would-be authoritarian makes it to power, democracies face a second critical test: will the autocratic leader subvert democratic institutions or be constrained by them?

Institutions alone are not enough to rein in elected autocrats. Constitutions must be defended—by political parties and organized citizens but also by democratic norms. Without robust norms, constitutional checks and balances do not serve as the bulwarks of democracy we imagine them to be. Institutions become political weapons, wielded forcefully by those who control them against those who do not.

This is how elected autocrats subvert democracy—packing and "weaponizing" the courts and other neutral agencies, buying off the media and the private sector (or bullying them into silence) and rewriting the rules of politics to tilt the playing field against opponents. The tragic paradox of the electoral route to authoritarianism is that democracy's assassins use the very institutions of democracy—gradually, subtly, and even legally—to kill it.

America failed the first test in November 2016, when we elected a president with a dubious allegiance to democratic norms.

Donald Trump's surprise victory was made possible not only by public disaffection but also by the Republican party's failure to keep an extremist demagogue within its own ranks from gaining the nomination.

How serious is the threat now? Many observers take comfort in our constitution, which was designed precisely to thwart and contain demagogues like Trump. Our Madisonian system of checks and balances has endured for more than two centuries. It survived the civil war, the great depression, the Cold War and Watergate. Surely, then, it will be able to survive Trump.

We are less certain. Historically, our system of checks and balances has worked pretty well—but not, or not entirely, because of the constitutional system designed by the founders. Democracies work best—and survive longer—where constitutions are reinforced by unwritten democratic norms.

Two basic norms have preserved America's checks and balances in ways we have come to take for granted: mutual toleration, or the understanding that competing parties accept one another as legitimate rivals, and forbearance, or the idea that politicians should exercise restraint in deploying their institutional prerogatives.

These two norms undergirded American democracy for most of the 20th century. Leaders of the two major parties accepted one another as legitimate and resisted the temptation to use their temporary control of institutions to maximum partisan advantage. Norms of toleration and restraint served as the soft guardrails of American democracy, helping it avoid the kind of partisan fight to the death that has destroyed democracies elsewhere in the world, including Europe in the 1930s and South America in the 1960s and 1970s.

Today, however, the guardrails of American democracy are weakening. The erosion of our democratic norms began in the 1980s and 1990s and accelerated in the 2000s. By the time Barack Obama became president, many Republicans in particular questioned the legitimacy of their Democratic rivals and had abandoned forbearance for a strategy of winning by any means necessary.

Trump may have accelerated this process, but he didn't cause it. The challenges facing American democracy run deeper. The weakening of our democratic norms is rooted in extreme partisan polarization—one that extends beyond policy differences into an existential conflict over race and culture.

America's efforts to achieve racial equality as our society grows increasingly diverse have fueled an insidious reaction and intensifying polarization. And if one thing is clear from studying breakdowns throughout history, it's that extreme polarization can kill democracies.

There are, therefore, reasons for alarm. Not only did Americans elect a demagogue in 2016, but we did so at a time when the norms that once protected our democracy were already coming unmoored.

But if other countries' experiences teach us that that polarization can kill democracies, they also teach us that breakdown is neither inevitable nor irreversible.

Many Americans are justifiably frightened by what is happening to our country. But protecting our democracy requires more than just fright or outrage. We must be humble and bold. We must learn from other countries to see the warning signs—and recognize the false alarms. We must be aware of the fateful missteps that have wrecked other democracies. And we must see how citizens have risen to meet the great democratic crises of the past, overcoming their own deep-seated divisions to avert breakdown.

History doesn't repeat itself. But it rhymes. The promise of history is that we can find the rhymes before it is too late.

Is Political Extremism a Significant Cause of Terrorism and Violent Crime in the US?

Overview: Extreme Polarization Could Contribute to Terrorist Conflict in the US

Luis De la Calle

Luis De la Calle is a fellow at the Center for Advanced Study in the Behavioral Sciences at Stanford University and associate professor in political science, Centro de Investigación y Docencia Económicas.

After President Joe Biden took office on Jan. 20, 2021, without any violent incidents, many in the United States and worldwide breathed a sigh of relief.

The respite may be brief. The ingredients that led an incensed pro-Trump mob to break into the Capitol and plant pipe bombs at other federal buildings on Jan. 6 remain.

Several US security experts say they now consider domestic extremism a greater threat to the country than international terror. According to my research on political violence, the US has all the elements that, combined, can produce a low-intensity terrorist conflict: extreme polarization and armed factions willing to break the law, in a wealthy democracy with a strong government.

Terror Can Thrive in Affluent Democracies Too

Chronic domestic terror is not the same as civil war.

In the modern era, civil wars usually take place in poor countries where the government is too weak and unstable to maintain control over a sprawling, often mountainous territory. Rebels take over swaths of the country and seek to replace the authorities in those areas. This is happening in Afghanistan, India and Nigeria, to name a few places.

In the United States, one of the world's more powerful nations, armed factions have a hard time permanently seizing land. Several

"US Could Face a Simmering, Chronic Domestic Terror Problem, Warn Security Experts," Luis De la Calle, The Conversation, January 21, 2021, https://theconversation .com/us-could-face-a-simmering-chronic-domestic-terror-problem-warn-security -experts-153375. Licensed under CC BY-4.0.

dramatic standoffs between fringe extremists and American authorities—including the 1993 Waco siege and the Bundy family's 41-day occupation of an Oregon wildlife refuge in 2016—ended poorly for the extremists.

A huge asymmetry of power between the state and armed factions prevents militants from openly battling to usurp its authority, as rebel groups like the Taliban do and the American Confederates did. It forces armed groups to act underground, hiding among the general population. Because democratic states cannot, at least on paper, openly violate human rights by systematically persecuting militants or torturing prisoners, underground armed rebels can thrive in democracies.

But operating in secret imposes heavy logistical constraints, my research shows.

It limits the number of operations they can sustain, meaning thinner ranks than full-fledged insurgencies and fewer overall fatalities than in civil wars. And although all rebels may dream of Che Guevara–style guerrilla adventures—heroically liberating "the people" from tyranny—in practice, militants working underground cannot avoid resorting to quintessential terrorist tactics such as bombs, shootings, bank robberies and kidnappings.

Take Italy's Red Brigades, for example. In the 1970s, this far-left organization aimed at overthrowing the capitalist system, but the Italian state was too strong. So the group resorted to terrorism. For two decades, the Red Brigades carried out a low-intensity campaign that killed perhaps 500 people, mainly with bombings and assassinations. They used violence as a strategy to raise consciousness about communism and provoke an insurrection.

In reaction to this communist violence, far-right groups like Nuclei Armati Rivoluzionari responded with indiscriminate attacks, including a no-warning 1980 train bombing in Bologna that killed 85 civilians. They sought to create a level of disruption so high that it would justify military intervention against the "enemies of the state"—a fascist coup d'état.

Both sides lost. There was no insurrection, no intervention.
Italian democracy prevailed.

Lone Wolf Terror

The US too, has experience with coordinated domestic terror.

Throughout the early 20th century, the Ku Klux Klan waged
vicious campaigns against Black Americans in the South. As the
tide of the civil rights movement ebbed in the late 1960s, radical
Marxists like the Weather Underground and the Black Liberation
Army emerged, using violence to oppose American military
intervention in Vietnam and push for racial equality.

Between 1969 and 1981, these two groups—one predominately
white, the other Black—conducted some 200 attacks, from bank
robberies to prison breaks. Fifteen people were killed, most of
them security officers.

The FBI engaged in heavy-handed repression, particularly
against Black militants. And Americans had scant interest in far
left-wing goals like helping the oppressed peoples of the world.
Both groups dwindled without much fanfare.

US history has also featured a smattering of fringe, lone wolf
terrorists, from the Unabomber on the left to the Atlanta Olympics
bomber Eric Rudolph on the right. This trend has recently
accelerated, with a deadly new massacre each year. Individual
white supremacists, in particular, have attacked immigrants and
people of color in Charleston, South Carolina, El Paso, Texas,
and beyond.

According to the Anti-Defamation League, which tracks hate
crimes, 2019 was one of the deadliest years for "domestic extremist-
related killings" since 1970, with 42 victims in 17 separate incidents.

Trump's Militias

Attacks characterized by lone wolf perpetrators have the
advantage of limiting legal scrutiny on the extremist milieu. But
with coordination, armed campaigns can scale up to do much
more damage.

To overcome the lone wolf stage, disparate militant groups must organize around a common theme that gives coherence to their violence. Trump's electoral defeat gave his armed followers a big one: the myth of a stolen election.

The Trump presidency emboldened a cabal of armed groups with a far-right agenda. Seeing their leader out of power will only grow this feeling of frustration. So will new repression of the far right, in the form of arrests, surveillance and social media clampdowns.

With Democrats controlling Washington and elections perceived as rigged, American far-right groups may believe further violence is the only way to counter what they see as federal overreach.

If they pursue terrorism, history shows their chances of succeeding are negligible. But this won't stop them from trying.

America Faces a Growing Threat from Right-Wing Extremists and Militia Groups

The Armed Conflict Location & Event Data Project

The Armed Conflict Location & Event Data Project (ACLED) is an organization dedicated to collecting and analyzing data on political violence around the world. ACLED maintains an up-to-date online crisis map and regularly publishes articles and other educational resources that are available and open for free use by the public.

Militia groups and other armed non-state actors pose a serious threat to the safety and security of American voters. Throughout the summer and leading up to the general election, these groups have become more assertive, with activities ranging from intervening in protests to organizing kidnapping plots targeting elected officials (CNN, 13 October 2020). Both the Department of Homeland Security and the Federal Bureau of Investigation have specifically identified extreme far right-wing and racist movements as a primary risk factor heading into November, describing the election as a potential "flashpoint" for reactionary violence (*The Nation*, 30 September 2020; *New York Times*, 6 October 2020).

ACLED collects and analyzes information about the actions of state, non-state, and sole perpetrator violence and demonstration activity. MilitiaWatch tracks, documents, and analyzes contemporary US militia movements, and provides reports connecting long-term militia trends to broader political events. ACLED and MilitiaWatch data indicate that right-wing militias have steadily ramped up their activities, and taken on an increasingly outsized profile within the national political environment.

This joint report reviews the latest data on right-wing militia organizations across the country, identifying the most active groups

"Standing By: Right-Wing Militia Groups & the US Election," The Armed Conflict Location & Event Data Project (ACLED). Reprinted by permission.

and mapping the locations most likely to experience heightened militia activity before, during, and after the election.

Although many US militias can be described as "latent" in that they threaten more violence than they commit, several recently organized militias are associated with a right-wing ideology of extreme violence towards communities opposed to their rhetoric and demands for dominance and control. The lack of open sanctions of these groups from public figures and select local law enforcement has given them space to operate, while concurrently allowing political figures to claim little direct responsibility for violent actions from which they hope to benefit.

ACLED has tracked the activities of over 80 militias across the US in recent months, the vast majority of which are right-wing armed groups. This report maps a subset of the most active right-wing militias, including "mainstream militias," which are those that work to align with US law enforcement (the Three Percenters, the Oath Keepers, the Light Foot Militia, the Civilian Defense Force, and the American Contingency); street movements that are highly active in brawls (the Proud Boys and Patriot Prayer); and highly devolved libertarian groups, which have a history of conflict and are skeptical of state forces (the Boogaloo Bois and People's Rights [Bundy Ranch]).

Analysis of a variety of drivers and barriers to militia activity allows for identification of high-risk locations ahead of the election. These include locations that have seen substantial engagement in anti-coronavirus lockdown protests as well as places where militias might have perceptions of "leftist coup" activities. Spaces where militias have been active in setting up recruitment drives or holding training for members are also at heightened risk, as are spaces where militia members cultivate personal relationships with police or law enforcement or where there might be a friendly attitude by law enforcement towards militia presence or activity. In the context of the upcoming election, swing states are also at heightened risk, in line with scholarship around election violence and unrest being more common in competitive spaces. And lastly, state capitals and "periphery" towns also remain important potential inflection points for violence, especially in more rural and suburban areas that have been particularly conducive to the foundation and regular activities of militia groups. Medium-population cities and suburban areas with centralized zones also serve as locations of major gravitational pull. Barriers to militia activity, meanwhile, can include locations with an overwhelming left-leaning population and/or large populations unsupportive of militias.

Based on these drivers and barriers, this report finds that capitals and peripheral towns, as well as medium-population cities and suburban areas with centralized zones, in Georgia, Michigan, Pennsylvania, Wisconsin, and Oregon are at highest risk of increased militia activity in the election and post-election period, while North Carolina, Texas, Virginia, California, and New Mexico are at moderate risk. Spotlights on each of these states offer a glimpse into recent trends associated with militia activity in each context in recent months.

Key Conclusions

There has been a major realignment of militia movements in the US from anti-federal government writ large to mostly supporting one candidate, thereby generally positioning the militia movement alongside a political party. This has resulted in the further entrenchment of a connection between these groups' identities and politics under the Trump administration, with the intention of preserving and promoting a limited and warped understanding of US history and culture.

These armed groups engage in hybrid tactics. They train for urban and rural combat while also mixing public relations, propaganda works, and "security operations" via both online and physical social platforms to engage those outside of the militia sphere. There is an increasing narrative and trend that groups are organizing to "supplement" the work of law enforcement or to place themselves in a narrowly defined "public protection" role in parallel with police departments of a given locale.

Ahead of the election, right-wing militia activity has been dominated by reactions to recent social justice activism like the Black Lives Matter movement, public health restrictions due to the ongoing coronavirus pandemic, and other perceived threats to the "liberty" and "freedoms" of these groups.

And right-wing militia groups are often highly competitive with one another, but many have coalesced around this period of heightened political tension, and have even brought Proud Boys and QAnon-linked groups into the fold. While some groups have indicated that they are receptive to calls for deescalation and conflict avoidance, they remain vulnerable to hardline elements that may work clandestinely towards violent action aimed at dominating public space around the election.

The January 6 Riot Proves That Extremism Is a Real Threat in America

Jaclyn Diaz and Rachel Treisman

Jaclyn Diaz is a breaking news reporter for NPR and previously served as reporter for Bloomberg Law. Rachel Treisman is a journalist with NPR.

Federal investigators say they have arrested several alleged members of extremist and white supremacist groups who participated in the Jan. 6 riot at the US Capitol building, including multiple participants in an alleged conspiracy.

People allegedly affiliated with organizations such as The Three Percenters, The Oath Keepers, Proud Boys, Texas Freedom Force, and other self-described Nazis and white supremacists were among the mob that stormed the US Capitol building, according to federal investigators.

Details of their arrests highlight how various extremist groups, with members throughout the country, coalesced to support Trump and his (disproven) claims that the November election was stolen. Law enforcement officials were able to track suspects down by using information gleaned from tipsters, social media posts shared by the accused, and news media coverage.

The Oath Keepers

Several people associated with the Oath Keepers are also facing charges related to the Capitol riot.

The FBI describes the Oath Keepers as a "large but loose organized collection of militia who believe that the federal government has been coopted by a shadowy conspiracy that is trying to strip American citizens of their rights."

"Members of Right-Wing Militias, Extremist Groups Are Latest Charged in Capitol Siege," by Jaclyn Diaz and Rachel Treisman, National Public Radio, January 19, 2021. Reprinted by permission.

Federal prosecutors are accusing Thomas Edward Caldwell, an apparent leader of the group, of helping to plan and coordinate the Jan. 6 storming of the US Capitol.

Caldwell, a 65-year-old resident of Clarke County, Va., was arrested on Tuesday on four charges including conspiracy to commit offense against the United States, according to the Justice Department.

Citing Facebook messages, an FBI affidavit supporting the criminal complaint alleges that Caldwell was "involved in planning and coordinating" the breach of the Capitol building.

On Jan. 1, for example, federal investigators said Caldwell sent a message helping arrange hotel accommodations for Jan. 5–7. That same day, another alleged member of the group sent Caldwell a message in which he called him "Commander" and said "Guess I'll be seeing you soon. Will probably call you tomorrow...mainly because...I like to know wtf plan is." On the evening of Jan. 6, Caldwell allegedly sent a flurry of Facebook messages about the day's riot, including a video that appears to have been taken inside the Capitol building. "I am such an instigator!" he allegedly wrote at one point.

"We need to do this at the local level," he wrote in another message, according to the investigators. "Lets [sic] storm the capitol in Ohio. Tell me when!"

According to the FBI, the Oath Keepers focuses on recruiting current and former military, law enforcement and first responders. The organization's name alludes to the oath sworn by members of the military and police to defend the Constitution "from all enemies, foreign and domestic."

It also describes video footage showing "8 to 10 individuals in paramilitary equipment aggressively approaching an entrance to the Capitol building." Prosecutors describe those individuals as moving "in an organized and practiced fashion," and based on their movements and clothing, believe them to be members of the Oath Keepers.

The FBI's affidavit identifies two other group members by name as having participated in the riot, Jessica Watkins and Donovan Crowl.

Watkins and Crowl, both of Champaign County, Ohio, were arrested Jan. 18.

Investigators say they are members of a group called the Ohio State Regular Militia, a local militia organization which pays dues to the Oath Keepers.

According to investigators, Watkins is a self-described commanding officer of the Ohio State Regular Militia. She shared videos online showing her and Crowl, at the Capitol, writing, "Yeah. We stormed the Capitol today. Teargassed, the whole, 9. Pushed our way into the Rotunda. Made it into the Senate even. The news is lying (even Fox) about the Historical Events we created today."

Another man allegedly linked to the Oath Keepers, but not explicitly named as part of the conspiracy, has also been arrested.

Jon Ryan Schaffer, of Columbus, Ind., a heavy metal musician and founder of the band Iced Earth, turned himself in to FBI agents in Indianapolis on Jan. 17.

An FBI affidavit says Schaffer has "long held far-right extremist views." He allegedly sprayed Capitol Police officers with bear spray as rioters pushed their way into the building. He is captured in videos and photos wearing a blue hooded sweatshirt under a tactical vest with a baseball cap that reads "Oath Keepers Lifetime Member."

Investigators say that when Schaffer took part in the Million MAGA March in Washington, D.C., in November, he told a reporter, "We're not going to merge into some globalist, communist system, it will not happen. There will be a lot of bloodshed if it comes down to that, trust me."

The Three Percenters

Guy Wesley Reffitt, of Wylie, Texas, was arrested Jan. 18 in his home state. He is facing charges of trespassing on restricted areas of the Capitol grounds and obstruction of justice.

Reffitt's wife told police that he is a member of the Texas Freedom Force, an extremist militia group, according to court documents.

The Texas Freedom Force, however, says on Twitter that the FBI has it wrong and that the group "is not a extremist militia (we are a nonprofit) & are far from extremist, the FBI didn't do their homework."

Reffitt's wife shared with authorities that he also belongs to the Three Percenters. The FBI says the group is born of the myth that only three percent of American colonists took up arms against the British during the American Revolution. Members of the group believe that a small force of well-armed and prepared members with a just cause can overthrow a tyrannical government.

Court documents say Reffitt threatened his son and daughter following his return home from the Jan. 6 siege at the Capitol. Reffitt's son said he saw his father bring home an AR-15 rifle and a Smith & Wesson pistol when he returned. Those firearms, among others, were retrieved by police when they searched his home.

Reffitt told his adult son that if he "crossed the line" and reported him to the police, Reffitt would have no option but to "do what he had to do," according to the affidavit. Reffitt's children told their mother what their father said to them. She confronted Reffitt and he said, "he was trying to protect the family, and if someone was a traitor then that's what's going to happen."

Robert Gieswein, from Woodland Park, Colo., is also believed to be a member of the Three Percenters, according to the FBI. He is facing charges in connection with an assault on a Capitol Police officer with pepper spray, a barricade surrounding the Capitol grounds, and a baseball bat. According to court documents, Gieswein posted a photo of himself on social media flashing the Three Percenters' sign and wearing clothing with the organization's logo.

The FBI says Gieswein also runs a private paramilitary group called the Woodland Wild Dogs, the patch of which he was seen wearing on the front of his tactical military vest in footage from the Capitol. In photos and videos, Gieswein is also seen wearing a helmet, goggles, and a black camouflage backpack.

Gieswein told reporters that "corrupt" politicians, of which he includes President-elect Joe Biden and Vice President-elect Kamala Harris, have sold the country out to the "Rothschilds and Rockefellers." The idea is a common conspiracy theory among far-right extremists who believe that a shadow force, including the famous European banking family and the American industrial and political dynasty, controls global currency.

Nazis and Proud Boys

Bryan Betancur, a self-professed white supremacist who has told law enforcement officers that he is a member of several white supremacist organizations, was caught on video during the riots. He was arrested Jan. 17.

Betancur, who was on probation when he went to the Capitol, has voiced "homicidal ideations, made comments about conducting a school shooting, and has researched mass shootings," according to court documents.

He is also engaged online in racist, violent extremist groups and has voiced support for James Fields, the neo-Nazi convicted of killing Heather Heyer during the 2017 Charlottesville, Va., "Unite the Right" rally, the FBI said. Betancur, who was arrested in Maryland on Jan. 17, is seen in videos of the Capitol attack flashing hand signals associated with white supremacy and wearing a Proud Boys t-shirt. The Proud Boys is a white nationalist organization with multiple US chapters.

Betancur, of Silver Spring, Md., also goes by the online aliases Bryan Clooney and Maximo Clooney, according to court documents.

Dominic Pezzola, a former Marine and Proud Boys member known as "Spaz" or "Spazzo" was arrested Jan. 15 in New York. Pezzola, who is from Rochester, N.Y., is seen in photos and videos of the Capitol riot wearing a black short-sleeved t-shirt with yellow, consistent with the "Proud Boys" logo, the FBI said.

A witness said Pezzola and others involved in the riots acknowledged that they would have "killed Vice President Mike Pence if given the chance."

Pence was at the Capitol in hiding during the attack.

Another individual charged is Timothy Hale-Cusanelli, a member of the US Army Reserve, who as a defense contractor at Naval Weapons Station Earle in New Jersey has a security clearance and access to a variety of munitions, according to court documents.

A police affidavit says Hale-Cusanelli, of Colts Neck, N.J., is "an avowed white supremacist and Nazi sympathizer" who posts videos on YouTube under the title the "Based Hermes Show," showcasing extreme political viewpoints.

A tipster told the FBI that Hale-Cusanelli had shared cell phone videos with the informant showing him at the Capitol building harassing police officers. Hale-Cusanelli also admitted to entering the Capitol and encouraging other members of the mob to "advance"—giving directions by voice and hand signals.

He was arrested Jan. 17 in New Jersey.

Guns Are a Way to Exercise Power

Lois Beckett and Josh Horwitz

Lois Beckett is a reporter for ProPublica and the Guardian. *Her work focuses on gun policy, criminal justice, and the far right in the United States. Josh Horwitz is the executive director of the Coalition to Stop Gun Violence and the Educational Fund to Stop Gun Violence. He is the author of the 2009 book* Guns, Democracy, and the Insurrectionist Idea *(Michigan University Press).*

Josh Horwitz has been an American gun control activist for nearly 30 years. In 2009, he co-wrote a book warning that the idea of armed revolt against the government was at the center of the US gun rights movement.

Now, after a year that has seen heavily armed men show up at state capitols in Virginia, Michigan, Idaho and elsewhere to confront Democratic lawmakers over gun control and coronavirus restrictions, more Americans are taking gun owners' rhetoric about "tyrants" seriously. Some of the same armed protesters who showed up at Michigan's state house and at a pro-gun rally this summer were charged last week with conspiring to kidnap Michigan's governor and put her on trial for tyranny.

Other members of the "boogaloo" movement have allegedly murdered law enforcement officers in California and plotted acts of violence across the country in hopes of sparking a civil war.

Horwitz spoke to the *Guardian* about how mainstream the idea of insurrection has become in American politics, and why lawmakers have failed to challenge it for decades.

The conversation has been condensed and edited for clarity.

"'Guns Are a Way to Exercise Power': How the Idea of Overthrowing the Government Became Mainstream," by Lois Beckett, Guardian News and Media Limited, October 18, 2020. Reprinted by permission.

You argue in your book that the idea of violent insurrection against the American government is at the heart of American gun culture. What do you mean by that?

There's a belief among some American gun owners that the second amendment is highly individualized and was placed in the constitution as an individual right to fight government tyranny. Therefore, each individual has the right to own whatever and however many weapons they want, free from any government interference. A licensing law or a universal background check law would mean the government knows who's got a gun. If you believe there's an individual right to insurrection, you can't have any gun laws.

The drive to purchase semi-automatic assault weapons, like AR-15s, those weapons are often not purchased for self-defense, but for fear of government tyranny.

When the NRA says, "Vote Freedom First," it's not "Vote self-defense first." They mean you get to decide when the government becomes tyrannical. The problem is that one person's tyranny is another's universal healthcare bill.

Is this concept of "insurrection" as the reason Americans should have unrestricted gun rights a very fringe idea?

It's not every gun owner. But this movement is way larger than people think. And guns are now seen by a large portion of that community as a tool for political dissent.

When National Rifle Association CEO Wayne LaPierre says things like, "The guys with the guns make the rules," or politicians and elected officials say, "We will rely on second amendment remedies," what they mean is that people with guns will, in fact, set the political agenda and settle political disputes. That is a profoundly undemocratic idea. As Abe Lincoln famously said, "Any appeal from the ballot box to the bullet box must fail." We are a country based on the rule of law. Guns don't make you a super citizen with the ability to make special rules or have special political influence because you happen to be armed.

Where does this "insurrectionary idea" come from? When did it take hold?

The idea that individuals have the right to fight against tyranny is as old as the republic. But you can trace the modern incarnation of this principle to the early 1990s, and the rise of the militia movement during Bill Clinton's presidency, when national gun violence prevention laws, including the assault weapons ban and background checks, were instituted. There's a path from Ruby Ridge and Waco [deadly standoffs between citizens and federal agents, both involving illegal gun charges] to the Oklahoma City bombing. The Michigan militia is where Timothy McVeigh, the Oklahoma City bomber, got this start. He was making his living at gun shows. He bought fully into the gun rights agenda, and he ended up killing a lot of kids. I started to pick up the resurgence of this idea in the mid-2000s, at the end of Bush's presidency and the beginning of Obama's presidency.

How does racism play into this idea of "insurrection" and its place in US politics?

There is a big racial element to this. White men, especially, are feeling that the political reins of power are pulling away from them, and their grip on power is falling away. Guns are a way to exercise power, let's face it. Power over policy. Power over people.

You first published *Guns, Democracy and the Insurrectionist Idea* in 2009. What kind of response did it get?

People didn't react the way that I hoped, by saying: this is going to be a big deal unless we move forcefully to oppose it. Instead, a lot of elected officials, including a lot of Democratic elected officials, acquiesced to the idea of an insurrectionary second amendment. People running for president in 2004 and 2008 would use lines like, "The second amendment isn't for hunting. It has to do with protecting ourselves, our homes, our families and our country from tyranny." Nobody followed up with: "What do you mean? You think it's OK to shoot politicians?"

This year, we saw the Michigan legislature taken over, the Idaho legislature taken over, and it's like—there's no opprobrium. There's a sort of, "boys will be boys" response.

Why has politicians' response to rhetoric about violent revolt been so muted?
I think there's the idea that if this really happened, the US army would just mow these people down. "Oh, it'd be suicide if they did that." But the US military should not be deployed in civilian places to begin with. What are we going to do, have tanks on our own soil? We're not going to do that. The other thing is that this movement is really well armed. There's a lot of firepower in civilian hands: .50 caliber sniper rifles, AR-15s, AK-47s.

If they really did it, it would be very, very complicated.

How significant are the numbers of US military members and police who personally believe in this insurrectionist idea themselves? This year, US military veterans and active duty service members have been charged in a number of violent plots, including some that were allegedly designed to spark a civil war.
There are some elements of law enforcement that are sympathetic to this. A lot are not, especially those in leadership. I have friends in the military, and, to many of them, this idea is complete anathema. But a lot of the demographics in the military are young white men who like guns. I do think the vast majority of law enforcement and the military will do their duty, but that doesn't mean that everyone will.

What shifts have you seen since 2009 in how insurrectionism is playing out?
There's been a huge change in the last four years, since Trump came to power. He doesn't condemn violence. What he said about Michigan governor Gretchen Whitmer was awful. When he's asked about a peaceful transition of power and he hedges, I believe it's because he thinks he has a private militia that will back him up.

The insurrectionist idea is about fighting government tyranny, but it would be especially dangerous if it became in service of particular officials, and that's what you're seeing now.

What's also changed: the amount of weapons that the boys have these days is obscene. The number of AR-15s and high-capacity magazines and assault weapons they have should scare anybody.

Are you worried that there could be a major insurrection against the US government?
Yes.

My fear is that there will be violence if the election is contested, or if it looks like Trump's losing. I worry that there will be efforts at intimidating election officials and voters.

I've always been concerned about the one-off person, the lone wolf who takes these ideas to the max. I am much more concerned now about organized efforts to subvert elections, democratic power, courts.

You issued a report focused on how states can ban gun-carrying at polling places. Are you concerned about what could happen on election day itself?
I don't think there's going to be widespread violence at the polls. I think there will be places where people with guns will attempt to intimidate voters, but not by shooting or anything like that, and I think those places will be relatively rare. It's really important that each polling place knows what their rights are, but I think there's been enough time to get them up to speed. I don't want people to be scared: the ultimate response to the insurrectionary second amendment is to go vote.

What do you think should be done now in response to all of this public conversation about insurrection?
Number one: there needs to be a clear public response, that people who exercise this "right" are not patriots, but traitors.

The second piece is a policy response. We need to limit access to assault weapons. As soon as legislatures open in 2021, they should ban guns at polling places. I would like to see them banning open carry everywhere. Peaceful protesters are now routinely intimidated by armed insurrectionists. The way they intimidate people is by openly carrying weapons. We have proved we can't handle that as a society.

And people who have the bully pulpit need to be careful not to endorse the idea of an insurrectionary second amendment. Even if you believe in an individual right to own a firearm, the purpose of that right cannot be to kill government officials.

Have you seen any tipping point in how Democratic politicians are now responding to this kind of insurrectionist rhetoric?
Let me be completely clear: the biggest problem is Republican elected officials, and the Republican who consistently use the insurrectionary idea and cheer on this type of behavior. While I wish Democrats would stand up and not just acquiesce, the Republican party has bought into a "second amendment remedies" idea that is now a danger, a grave danger, to America.

The Republican elected officials in Virginia thought the gun rights march on the state capitol was the greatest thing since sliced bread. There are plenty of Republican officials who just think this is great.

Americans Can No Longer Ignore the Threat Posed by the Extreme Right

Alexander Hinton

Alexander Hinton is Distinguished Professor of Anthropology at Rutgers University. He also serves as director of the Center for the Study of Genocide and Human Rights and UNESCO chair on genocide prevention at Rutgers. He is the author of several books on genocide, torture, and global political violence.

In the wake of the mob incursion that took over the US Capitol on Jan. 6, it's clear that many people are concerned about violence from far-right extremists. But they may not understand the real threat.

The law enforcement community is among those who have failed to understand the true nature and danger of far-right extremists. Over several decades, the FBI and other federal authorities have only intermittently paid attention to far-right extremists. In recent years, they have again acknowledged the extent of the threats they pose to the country. But it's not clear how long their attention will last.

Clearly the US Capitol Police underestimated the threat on Jan. 6. Despite plenty of advance notice and offers of help from other agencies, they were caught totally unprepared for the mob that took over the Capitol.

While researching my forthcoming book, *It Can Happen Here: White Power and the Rising Threat of Genocide in the US*, I discovered that there are five key mistakes people make when thinking about far-right extremists. These mistakes obscure the extremists' true danger.

"US Capitol Mob Highlights 5 Reasons Not to Underestimate Far-Right Extremists," by Alexander Hinton, The Conversation, October 30, 2020. https://theconversation.com /us-capitol-mob-highlights-5-reasons-not-to-underestimate-far-right-extremists-148610. Licensed under CC BY-ND 4.0.

1. Some Have White Supremacist Views, but Others Don't

When asked to condemn white supremacists and extremists at the first presidential debate, President Donald Trump floundered, then said, "Give me a name." His Democratic challenger Joe Biden offered, "The Proud Boys."

Not all far-right extremists are militant white supremacists.

White supremacy, the belief in white racial superiority and dominance, is a major theme of many far-right believers. Some, like the Ku Klux Klan and neo-Nazis, are extremely hardcore hate groups.

Others, who at times identify themselves with the term "alt-right," often mix racism, anti-Semitism and claims of white victimization in a less militant way. In addition, there are what some experts have called the "alt-lite," like the Proud Boys, who are less violent and disavow overt white supremacy even as they promote white power by glorifying white civilization and demonizing nonwhite people including Muslims and many immigrants.

There is another major category of far-right extremists who focus more on opposing the government than they do on racial differences. This so-called "patriot movement" includes tax protesters and militias, many heavily armed and a portion from military and law enforcement backgrounds. Some, like the Hawaiian-shirt-wearing Boogaloos, seek civil war to overthrow what they regard as a corrupt political order.

2. They Live in Cities and Towns Across the Nation and Even the Globe

Far-right extremists are in communities all across America.

The KKK, often thought of as centered in the South, has chapters from coast to coast. The same is true of other far-right extremist groups.

Far-right extremism is also global, a point underscored by the 2011 massacre in Norway and the 2019 New Zealand mosque attack, both of which were perpetrated by people claiming to resist "white genocide." The worldwide spread led the U.N. to recently issue a global alert about the "growing and increasing transnational threat" of right-wing extremism.

3. Many Are Well Organized, Educated and Social Media Savvy

Far-right extremists include people who write books, wear sport coats and have advanced degrees. For instance, in 1978 a physics professor turned neo-Nazi wrote a book that has been called the "bible of the racist right." Other leaders of the movement have attended elite universities.

Far-right extremists were early users of the internet and now thrive on social media platforms, which they use to agitate, recruit and organize. The 2017 "Unite the Right" rally in Charlottesville revealed how effectively they could reach large groups and mobilize them into action.

Platforms like Facebook and Twitter have recently attempted to ban many of them. But the alleged Michigan kidnappers' ability to evade restrictions by simply creating new pages and groups has limited the companies' success.

4. They Were Here Long Before Trump and Will Remain Here Long After

Many people associate far-right extremism with the rise of Trump. It's true that hate crimes, anti-Semitism and the number of hate groups have risen sharply since his campaign began in 2015. And the QAnon movement—called both a "collective delusion" and a "virtual cult"—has gained widespread attention.

But far-right extremists were here long before Trump.

The history of white power extremism dates back to slave patrols and the post–Civil War rise of the KKK. In the 1920s, the KKK had millions of members. The following decade saw the rise of Nazi sympathizers, including 15,000 uniformed "Silver Shirts" and a 20,000-person pro-Nazi rally at Madison Square Garden in New York City in 1939.

While adapting to the times, far-right extremism has continued into the present. It's not dependent on Trump, and will remain a threat regardless of his public prominence.

5. They Pose a Widespread and Dire Threat, with Some Seeking Civil War

Far-right extremists often appear to strike in spectacular "lone wolf" attacks, like the Oklahoma City federal building bombing in 1995, the mass murder at a Charleston church in 2015 and the Pittsburgh synagogue shooting in 2018. But these people are not alone.

Most far-right extremists are part of larger extremist communities, communicating by social media and distributing posts and manifestos.

Their messages speak of fear that one day, whites may be outnumbered by nonwhites in the US, and the idea that there is a Jewish-led plot to destroy the white race. In response, they prepare for a war between whites and nonwhites.

Thinking of these extremists as loners risks missing the complexity of their networks, which brought as many as 13 alleged plotters together in the planning to kidnap Michigan's governor.

Together, these misconceptions about far-right extremist individuals and groups can lead Americans to underestimate the dire threat they pose to the public. Understanding them, by contrast, can help people and experts alike address the danger, as the election's aftermath unfolds.

Preventative Political Policing Has a Long History in the United States

Chip Gibbons

Chip Gibbons is a writer for Jacobin *magazine and policy director of Defending Rights & Dissent. His work focuses on domestic political surveillance and the American national security state.*

On June 26, Attorney General William Barr announced the creation of a new task force on "violent anti-government extremists." Made up of representatives of the US Attorney's Office, the Federal Bureau of Investigation (FBI) and "other relevant components," the task force comes in the midst of a nationwide uprising against racism and police violence. While Barr's initial statement cited as examples of "violent anti-government extremists" both the right-wing "Boogaloo" movement and "Antifa," the taskforce is primarily a right-wing reaction to racial justice protests erupting across the country.

This development is in keeping with the FBI's history of spying on nearly every major social movement, from the anti-Vietnam war and civil rights movements, to Occupy Wall Street and Black Lives Matter. And it comes as Barr and Trump have repeatedly tried to turn "Antifa," or anti-fascist ideology, into an all-purpose boogeyman. Within this context, the creation of the new task force on violent anti-government extremism should be viewed as a dangerous act aimed at policing the politics of racial justice protesters.

The Problem with Preventive Political Policing

The task force is not just tasked with prosecuting violent anti-government extremists who engage in domestic terrorism, but preventing these groups or individuals from engaging in violence

"Barr's New Task Force Is a Blatant Attempt to Target Racial Justice Protesters," by Chip Gibbons, *In These Times*, July 10, 2020. Reprinted by permission.

before it occurs and to "ultimately eliminate it as a threat to public safety and the rule of law." While preventing violence before it occurs may sound noble, preventive policing is fraught with abuse. After all, it inherently involves law enforcement action or intrusive intelligence gathering against people who have not committed any crime based on the notion that law enforcement and intelligence can successfully pinpoint potential criminals.

Mike German, a former FBI agent and current fellow with the Brennan Center for Justice's Liberty & National Security Program, told *In These Times* the claim that "law enforcement or intelligence officers can accurately predict who will engage in criminal behavior in the future is a dubious assumption." Such a preventive framework, says German, "justifies broad law enforcement or intelligence activities as necessary to serve the laudatory goal of preventing crime where the evidence of success— no crime occurring—justifies the action taken even when there is no evidence the tactics prevented the crime rather than that the prediction that a crime would occur was false."

The language about prevention is also a red flag for those familiar with the FBI's use of radicalization theory, which has been central to its Countering Violent Extremism initiative, a counter terrorism program aimed at identifying individuals likely to become terrorists. Radicalization theory posits that one becomes a terrorist by adopting ideas the FBI deems radical or extremist. This theory rests on the premise that there is set path by which one radicalizes into becoming violent. As this path has identifiable points, knowing those points allows to law enforcement and intelligence to intervene before an individual is a full fledged terrorist.

The underlying methodological assumptions of this theory and the idea that there is a set path to terrorism are widely disputed. Civil libertarians also point out that political speech the government deems radical or extremist is still protected by the First Amendment. Claiming that espousing political views disfavored by the government is the first step to becoming a terrorist opens the door to political surveillance.

This is apparent in an online game created in 2016 by the FBI to
teach teenagers how to prevent violent extremism. In one scenario,
students are given a list of fictional social media posts and asked
to identity the one "most likely a violent extremist looking for new
recruits." The correct answer is a post asking if anyone is interested
in joining him at "that awful animal testing lab" to "send them a
'powerful' message and shut them down once and for all." It's a
vague post that could refer to a destructive act, but it could also
refer to mere political protest. The message it sends to students is
clear: certain forms of political speech are suspicious. (The initial
version of this game used as an example of reportable behavior
a student with a Muslim-sounding name discussing an overseas
trip. After civil rights groups objected to the game's promotion
of racial profiling, this specific example was changed. Civil rights
groups still objected to the game on grounds that it promoted
racial and religious profiling.

This game isn't the only reason for concern. A 2010 FBI primer
on anarchist extremism describes it as encompassing "a variety
of ideologies, including anti-capitalism, anti-globalism and anti-
urbanization." In 2001 congressional testimony about the terrorist
threat posed by "left-wing and Puerto Rican extremist groups," the
FBI director defined those groups as professing "a revolutionary
socialist doctrine and view themselves as protectors of the people
against the 'dehumanizing effects' of capitalism and imperialism."

If political speech leads to one becoming a terrorist, then
preventive policing based in the radicalization framework means
policing political speech. As German told *In These Times*, "History
shows the government often posits that political activities and
speech are precursors or indicators of future violence, so the whole
prevention framework serves to justify the suppression of political
opposition rather than crime."

The focus on not just prosecutions, but eliminating the threat
of extremism, is evocative of one the darkest chapters in the
FBI's history. While the FBI has a long track record of political
surveillance, from 1956 to 1971, the FBI went a step further. Under

the Counterintelligence Program (COINTELPRO), the FBI carried out what the Church Committee, the landmark Senate investigation into US intelligence operations, labeled a domestic covert action against American citizens viewed as threatening "the existing political and social order." COINTELPRO drew upon "techniques of wartime" designed to counter hostile foreign agents and applied them to domestic political movements.

The FBI created COINTELPRO in 1956 because it was frustrated with what it perceived as a lack of law enforcement avenues to destroy the Communist Party. Fearing it was unable to prosecute individuals whose speech the FBI considered a national security threat, it moved into actively trying to "neutralize" or "disrupt" these groups. As historian Ellen Schrecker succinctly put it, FBI Director J. Edgar "and his men decided to use dirty tricks instead of criminal prosecutions to neutralize the party."

COINTELPRO quickly expanded beyond the Communist Party, but the initiation of new operations was always premised on the FBI's belief that, for whatever reason, prosecution and normal law enforcement avenues were foreclosed when it came to thwarting the movement in question. As a result, COINTELPRO by its very design often targeted entirely lawful First Amendment-protected political organizing for neutralization.

Targeting Racial Justice Protesters

The task force's stated target gives further cause for concern that it will allow the FBI to ramp up its history of political policing. The phrase "anti-government extremism" entered the FBI lexicon as part of a shift in how the FBI defines domestic terrorism. In 2017, the FBI claimed it recognized the existence of nine "persistent extremist movements": "white supremacy, black identities, militia, sovereign citizens, anarchists, abortion, animal rights, environmental rights and Puerto Rican Nationalism." (Abortion extremism, per the FBI, refers not just to anti-choice actors, but pro-choice ones, as well.) The term Black Identity Extremism, which was revealed initially when an FBI intelligence assessment was leaked to Foreign Policy, garnered significant backlash. Faced with Congressional scrutiny, FBI director Christopher Wray told Congress the bureau no longer used that term. Instead, the FBI now recognized four categories of domestic terrorism: racially motivated violent extremism, anti-government/anti-authority extremism, animal rights/environmental extremism, and abortion extremism.

Gone was not only Black Identity Extremism, but white supremacist, anarchist, sovereign citizen, militias, and Puerto Rican extremism. Or at least the terms were gone.

A second leak of FBI documents shows that the definition of Black Identity Extremism had hardly been eliminated, but incorporated wholesale into racially motivated violent extremism. Lawmakers criticized this category for merging Black Identity Extremism and white supremacy. A letter signed by seven US senators states that doing so creates not just a false equivalency, but "obfuscates the white supremacist threat."

The terms "anti-government" or "anti-authority extremism" works according to the same logic. Right-wing militias and anarchist protesters are brought together in one unified category.

The obfuscatory nature of the FBI's new domestic terrorism categories is on full display with Barr's task force on violent anti-government extremism. While it's clear Barr is targeting "antifa," a catch-all for leftwing protesters, he is also able to pretend he is focusing on rightwing groups.

This isn't the first time antifa has been mentioned. In late 2017, director Christopher Wray, when asked by Congress if the FBI was investigating "antifa," explained that antifa or anti-fascism was a political ideology. The FBI did not, according to Wray, investigate ideology. The FBI, however, had opened numerous "anarchist extremism" investigations into individuals supposedly motivated to violent action "by a kind of an antifa ideology," he explained. The FBI's own primer on the domestic terrorism threat of anarchist extremism references this group's and anti-globalist ideologies. This is all firmly within the jurisdiction of a task force focusing on the sinister sounding violent anti-government extremism.

A New Red Scare?

Barr isn't hiding the ball: He's attacked antifa and the left by name. In a press conference on George Floyd protests, Barr declared "in many places it appears the violence is planned, organized, and driven by anarchic and left extremist groups, far-left extremist groups, using antifa-like tactics."

This is clearly the language of a Red Scare. And it isn't just Barr who's parroting it.

Rep. Matt Gaetz (R-Fla.) tweeted "Black Lives Matter is a Marxist movement." On the floor of the house, Rep. Andy Biggs (R-Ariz.) mused that the current situation "reminds me an awful lot of" the Bolshevik Revolution. Sen. Tom Cotton (R-Ark.), who has called for the military to be used against protesters, proclaimed, "Look at what's happening in Seattle. Revolutionaries, anarchists have taken over city government buildings." In the same piece, he claimed some on the left had "adopted the spirit of a Jacobin mob in the French Revolution, the Reign of Terror trying to completely erase our culture and our history."

And then there's Trump.

An executive order issued on June 26, supposedly to protect statues and monuments, states, "Many of the rioters, arsonists and left-wing extremists who have carried out and supported these acts have explicitly identified themselves with ideologies—such as Marxism—that call for the destruction of the United States system of government. Anarchists and left-wing extremists have sought to advance a fringe ideology that paints the United States of America as fundamentally unjust and have sought to impose that ideology on Americans through violence and mob intimidation."

Standing before Mt. Rushmore on July 3, Trump decried "far-left fascism" and warned of a "left-wing cultural revolution" "designed to overthrow the American Revolution."

The following day, at a Fourth of July "Salute to America," Trump carried on with similar themes, declaring, "We are now in the process of defeating the radical left, the Marxists, the anarchists, the agitators, the looters, and people who in many instances have absolutely no clue what they are doing."

While Trump has resorted to these incendiary denouncements of racial justice protesters, this rhetoric did not entirely begin with the nationwide uprising against police brutality. At the 2019 State of the Union address, Trump proclaimed America would "never be a socialist country," a claim he has again made at campaign rallies. But amid escalating Covid-19 deaths, mass unemployment and a looming eviction crisis, Trump appears to be ratcheting up his rhetoric. A nationwide uprising against police racism and an insurgent democratic socialist movement has challenged the political consensus. With sinking approval ratings, Trump is clearly desperate. Trump and the far-right forces that have chosen him as their avatar are clearly trying to retain their grip on power with bombastic, Red Scare rhetoric.

The FBI has always been central to Red Scares in the United States. The height of the early 20th century Red Scare came when the FBI's newly minted intelligence division, headed by its future director J. Edgar Hoover, gathered dossiers on radicals and carried out the Palmer Raids. During the Cold War, the FBI was the bureaucratic heart of the McCarthy era. Barr's creation of the task force on violent anti-government extremism is clearly part and parcel of this legacy. It will be used to go after political opponents and police the politics of the left. Reining in the FBI's political policing is not only vital to protecting civil liberties, but defending the movement for racial justice it is targeting.

Socialist Perceptions of the Far Left Is the New Red Scare

David Smith

David Smith is Washington correspondent for the Guardian, *where he previously served as Africa correspondent. He appears regularly on CNN, NPR, and the BBC.*

It came from abroad and infected America. It can spread from person to person and is potentially fatal. When symptoms emerge, it may already be too late.

The virus of socialism has broken out again, the biggest annual gathering of US conservatives was told this week, and it puts everything they hold dear at risk.

The leftwing ideology poses a bigger threat to the economy than the rampant coronavirus, Larry Kudlow, the economic adviser to Donald Trump, told the Conservative Political Action Conference (CPAC).

"The virus is not going to sink the American economy," he said at the National Harbor near Washington. "What is, or could, sink the American economy is the socialism coming from our friends on the other side of the aisle. That's the biggest fear that I have today."

Claiming that "the Lord loves free enterprise," Kudlow, who shared a stage with the president's daughter Ivanka, added: "I don't want to be snarky. I don't even want to be political. We will have it out this year: America versus socialism."

"America vs socialism" was the official theme of this year's CPAC, a slogan stamped all over the convention centre. The agenda included sessions entitled "Socialism: Wrecker of Nations and Destroyer of Societies," "Socialism and the Great Awokening" and "Prescription for Failure: The Ills of Socialised Medicine."

"'America v Socialism': Conservatives Rage Against the Left and Plot New Red Scare," by David Smith, Guardian News and Media Limited, March 1, 2020. Reprinted by permission.

Before Trump's speech on Saturday in an opulent ballroom, a parody SNN—"Socialist News Network"—studio was set up on the main stage for a routine that included mockery of Democrats and teenage climate activist Greta Thunberg. Host Jesse Kelly promised to be back to bring more news "from our studio to your breadline."

As a framing of the upcoming election battle, it might also have been described as "the return of the red scare." Seventy years after Republican senator Joseph McCarthy alleged that hundreds of communists had infiltrated the US government, launching a witch hunt that reached into the army and Hollywood, there was fresh fearmongering about Democrats in general and Bernie Sanders in particular.

CPAC organiser Matt Schlapp, chairman of the American Conservative Union, told attendees: "America versus socialism: it's a very intended theme. Our view is it's not capitalism versus socialism because socialism isn't just about economics. Socialism, we believe, gets to the very core of violating the dignity of the individual human being that has God given rights. And that's got us pretty fired up."

Mike Lee, a Republican senator from Utah, said: "Socialism is as socialism does. One of the things that differentiates Bernie Sanders from others is that he actually acknowledges he's a socialist. He's far from the only one in the United States Senate, sadly enough."

Lee added darkly: "They're talking about having the government become your healthcare provider, your banker, your nanny, your watchdog. Having the government lie to you and spy on you and requiring the government to force you to work months out of every single year. In a word, the Democratic party has become the party of socialism. I don't think we're ready for that and I know you aren't."

Trump supporters wandering the corridors agreed that the perceived threat of socialism will be a motivating factor on election day. Many characterised it as big government promising something for nothing, raising taxes and curtailing freedoms. They pointed to examples of poverty in Cuba and Venezuela and tyranny in China and the Soviet Union.

Claude O'Donovan, 81, remembered listening to the McCarthy hearings on the radio. "Communism was a muddy thing at the time," he said. "He didn't have the charisma to make the argument."

Now he takes the Democrats' shift to the left seriously. "Today it's a real threat. Bernie Sanders can say he's a 'democratic socialist' but that's just an acronym for communist. It's communism without a gun. In this day and age, I would never have thought we'd have socialism become so dominant in the country."

O'Donovan, from Aiken, South Carolina, turned up wearing a "Trump" cap and a Santa Claus costume—a hobby of his. "Santa gave things at Christmas to celebrate the birth of Jesus Christ. These people want us to give everything from cradle to grave and it can't be done. We can't print money."

What if Sanders is elected?

"We would crash almost immediately. It would be disastrous."

Asked the same question, Ronald Solomon, 60, a retailer of Trump merchandise from Las Vegas, replied: "The guy's a certified nut and the world would be hurt. The last place to go for real freedom would be destroyed by a radical socialist. Any place they've decided to go down that road has resulted in a stagnating middle class, a collapse of business and people forced to break into zoos to feed themselves."

Sanders' brand of democratic socialism is more Scandinavian than Soviet, seeking to expand publicly funded education and healthcare and tackle inequality. He has been endorsed by Congresswoman Alexandria Ocasio-Cortez, 30, and dominates among young Democratic voters.

Victoria Spiotto, a 21-year-old student from Ashburn, Virginia, was having none of it. "For me, socialism is a completely destructive ideology and system," she said. "I think a lot of young people are ready for it but most Americans don't trust it. You have people from Venezuela and Cuba who speak out about it and tell the truth of the situation."

Numerous students were sporting T-shirts that said, "Kiss me, I'm a capitalist" coupled with images of shamrocks ahead of St. Patrick's Day. Among them was Salicia Bayes, 21, from Lansing in Michigan. "I have a lot of friends from Venezuela and just hearing their stories is terrifying," she said. "Even a lot of people in the Democratic party are not going to vote for Sanders."

Others questioned how Sanders would pay for his ambitious reforms. Robert Douglas, 86, a neurologist from Pensacola, Florida, wearing a "Keep America great" cap, said: "You can't justify Medicare for all: it will cost $30tn. What about the green new deal? We're talking about $60tn for that. JFK was the last moderate Democrat in my lifetime: he was not for big government."

On Friday, British rightwing politician Nigel Farage urged attendees to donate to Sanders' campaign, predicted that his nomination would guarantee victory for Trump and could enable Republicans to regain the House. Some agreed with that analysis. Shea Justice, 19, a student from Arlington, Massachusetts, said: "We're calling it right now: Bernie Sanders is the next Jeremy Corbyn."

Although Sanders made for an obvious and satisfying target, he was seen as symptomatic of a deeper shift in the Democratic party. A former New York police officer who goes by the name of Grizzly Joe said: "They're all just different degrees of socialism, saying the same stuff in a different way. At least Bernie is honest about it. They want free this, free that. They're telling their base, whoever that is—the morons that vote for them—that we'll give you free stuff. It's not physically possible."

In a speech on Thursday, Vice-President Mike Pence summed up: "Today's Democratic party has been taken over by radical leftists who want higher taxes, open borders and late-term abortion. There are no moderates in this Democratic field. Every other one of the Democrats running for president embraces Bernie's democratic socialism."

Evidence Shows That the Extreme Left in America Is Mostly Nonviolent

Lois Beckett

Lois Beckett is a reporter for ProPublica and the Guardian. *Her work focuses on gun policy, criminal justice, and the far right in the United States. She has received the Deadline Award and a NABJ Salute to Excellence Award in investigative journalism.*

Editor's note: Since this piece was published in July 2020, the data has changed: domestic terrorism experts now link one homicide in the US to a self-described anti-fascist, the first such killing in 25 years.

Donald Trump has made warnings about the threat of antifa and "far-left fascism" a central part of his re-election campaign. But in reality leftwing attacks have left far fewer people dead than violence by rightwing extremists, new research indicates, and antifa activists have not been linked to a single murder in decades.

A new database of nearly 900 politically motivated attacks and plots in the United States since 1994 includes just one attack staged by an anti-fascist that led to fatalities. In that case, the single person killed was the perpetrator.

Over the same time period, American white supremacists and other rightwing extremists have carried out attacks that left at least 329 victims dead, according to the database.

More broadly, the database lists 21 victims killed in leftwing attacks since 2010, and 117 victims of rightwing attacks in that same period—nearly six times as much. Attacks inspired by the Islamic State and similar jihadist groups, in contrast, killed 95 people since 2010, slightly fewer than rightwing extremists, according to the data set. More than half of these victims died in a single attack on a gay nightclub in Orlando, Florida, in 2016.

"Anti-Fascists Linked to Zero Murders in the US in 25 Years," by Lois Beckett, Guardian News and Media Limited, July 27, 2020. Reprinted by permission.

"Leftwing Violence Has Not Been a Major Terrorism Threat"

The database was assembled by researchers at the Center for Strategic and International Studies (CSIS), a centrist thinktank, and reviewed by the *Guardian*.

Its launch comes as Trump administration officials have echoed the president's warnings of a violent "leftwing" revolution. "Groups of outside radicals and agitators are exploiting the situation to pursue their own separate, violent and extremist agenda," the attorney general, William Barr, said amid nationwide protests following the death of George Floyd. A new justice department taskforce on violent anti-government extremists listed "antifa" as a major threat, while making no mention of white supremacy.

Defining which violent incidents constitute politically motivated acts of terrorism, and trying to sort political violence into leftwing and rightwing categories, is inherently messy and debatable work. This is particularly true in the US, where highly publicized mass shootings are common, and some have no clear political motivation at all.

Stated political motives for violent attacks often overlap with other potential factors, including life crises, anger issues, a history of violent behavior and, in some cases, serious mental health conditions.

While researchers sometimes disagree on how to categorize the ideology of specific attacks, multiple databases that track extremist violence, including data maintained by the Anti-Defamation League, and from journalists at the Center for Investigative Reporting, have found the same trend: It's violent rightwing attacks, not "far-left" violence, that presents the greater deadly threat to Americans today.

"Leftwing violence has not been a major terrorism threat," said Seth Jones, a counter-terrorism expert who led the creation of CSIS's dataset.

Categorizing "Leftwing" Extremist Attacks

Most of the deadly extremist attacks the CSIS researchers categorized as "leftwing" were killings of police officers by black men, many of them US military veterans, who described acting out of anger or retribution for police killings of black Americans.

These shooting attacks include the murder of two police officers in New York City in 2014, after Michael Brown and Eric Garner's killings; and the murders of five officers in Dallas, Texas, and three officers in Baton Rouge, Louisiana, in 2016.

Some of the gunmen who killed police had connections to black nationalist groups, which extremism researchers at CSIS and elsewhere said they typically categorize as leftwing, largely because in the 1960s, influential black nationalist groups like the Black Panther party were anti-capitalist and considered part of the New Left.

Making that categorization is less straightforward today, some researchers acknowledge, since some prominent black nationalist organizations express homophobic, misogynistic and antisemitic views, values that set them in opposition to the current American left.

Mark Pitcavage, a senior fellow at the ADL's Center on Extremism, noted that Gavin Eugene Long, who staged an attack on police in Baton Rouge, had ties to black nationalism and was also part of an offshoot of the sovereign citizens movement, an anti-government ideology that is typically categorized as rightwing.

In several of the high-profile leftwing attacks included in the CSIS list the only fatality was the perpetrator. A mass shooting attack on a group of congressional Republicans during a baseball practice outside of Washington, DC, in 2017 left the Republican congressman Steve Scalise seriously injured, and three other people shot.

The gunman, James Hodgkinson, 66, was the only one killed in the attack. Hodgkinson had deliberately targeted Republicans and had expressed disgust with Trump.

Many of the other leftwing attacks or plots in the CSIS database, including by anarchists, environmental groups and others, resulted in no deaths at all. Often, leftwing plots, particularly by animal rights activists, have targeted businesses or buildings, "and their primary weapons have been incendiaries designed to create fires or destroy infrastructure—not kill people," said Jones, the researcher who led the creation of the data set.

The one deadly anti-fascist attack listed in the database occurred in July 2019, when Willem von Spronsen, a 69-year-old white man, was shot dead by police outside an Ice detention center in Tacoma, Washington. Authorities said von Spronsen had been throwing molotov cocktails, setting flares, that he set a car on fire and that he had a rifle. Local activists told media outlets they believed he had been trying to destroy buses parked outside the facility that were used to transport people who were being deported.

Von Spronsen, who had previously been arrested at a protest outside the detention center, was involved in a contentious divorce, and both a friend and his ex-wife had described him as suicidal. In a letter he wrote to friends before his death, Von Spronsen called detention centers "concentration camps" and said he wanted to take action against evil, BuzzFeed News reported. "I am antifa," he reportedly wrote.

No one was harmed in the attack except Von Spronsen, according to media reports.

Researchers who monitor extremist groups at the Anti-Defamation League and the Global Project Against Hate and Extremism said they, too, were not aware of a single murder linked to an American anti-fascist in the last 20 to 25 years.

Heidi Beirich, a co-founder of the Global Project Against Hate and Extremism, said some leftwing groups were known for more radical and violent tactics in the 1960s, adding: "It's just not the case today."

Mark Pitcavage said he knew of only one killing, 27 years ago, that might potentially be classified as connected to anti-fascist activism: the shooting of a racist skinhead, Eric Banks, by an anti-racist skinhead, John Bair, in Portland, Oregon, in 1993.

"A False Equivalence"

Given the discrepancies between the deadly toll of leftwing and rightwing violence, American law enforcement agencies have long faced criticism for failing to take the threat of white supremacist violence seriously, while at the same time overstating the risks posed by leftwing protesters. After a violent rally in California in 2016, law enforcement officers worked with neo-Nazis to build criminal cases against anti-fascist protesters, while not recommending charges against neo-Nazis for stabbing the anti-fascists.

Antifa activists have been the targets of domestic terror attacks by white supremacists, including in a terror plot early this year, in which law enforcement officials alleged that members of the neo-Nazi group the Base had planned to murder a married couple in Georgia they believed were anti-fascist organizers.

"Antifa is not going around murdering people like rightwing extremists are. It's a false equivalence," said Beirich.

"I've at times been critical of antifa for getting into fights with Nazis at rallies and that kind of violence, but I can't think of one case in which an antifa person was accused of murder," she added.

The new CSIS database only includes attacks through early May 2020, and does not yet list incidents connected with the massive national protests against police violence after Minneapolis police killed George Floyd, including the killings of two California law enforcement officers by a man authorities say was linked to the rightwing "boogaloo" movement.

Today, Jones said, "the most significant domestic terrorism threat comes from white supremacists, anti-government militias and a handful of individuals associated with the 'boogaloo' movement that are attempting to create a civil war in the United States."

Daily interpersonal violence and state violence pose a much greater threat to Americans than any kind of extremist terror attack. More than 100,000 people have been killed in gun homicides

in the United States in the past decade, according to estimates
from the Centers for Disease Control and Prevention. US police
officers shoot nearly 1,000 Americans to death each year. Black
Americans are more than twice as likely to be shot by the police
as white Americans, according to analysis by the *Washington Post*
and the *Guardian*.

But the president's rhetoric about "antifa" violence has
dangerous consequences, not just for anti-fascists, but for any
Americans who decide to protest, some activists said.

Yvette Felarca, a California-based organizer and anti-fascist
activist, said she saw Trump's claims about antifa violence,
particularly during the George Floyd protests, as a message to
his "hardcore" supporters that it was appropriate to attack people
who came out to protest.

"It's his way of saying to his supporters: 'Yeah, go after them.
Beat them or kill them to the point where they go back home and
stay home afraid,'" Felarca said.

The Divide Caused by Political Sectarianism Can Be Bridged

Clark Merrefield

Clark Merrefield joined the Journalist's Resource in 2019 after working as a reporter for Newsweek *and the* Daily Beast, *as a researcher and editor on three books related to the Great Recession, and as a federal government communications strategist.*

It hardly bears rehashing that Democrats and Republicans view the 2020 general election in moralistic, good-versus-evil terms. Case in point: An Oct. 19 survey from the nonprofit, nonpartisan Public Religion Research Institute finds 78% of Democratic respondents think the Republican Party has been overtaken by racists while 81% of Republicans think the Democratic Party has been overtaken by socialists. The survey interviewed about 2,500 randomly selected adults across all 50 states and the District of Columbia.

Political scientists in recent years have used various terms to describe America's deep political divide, including "affective polarization," "social polarization" and "tribalism." The authors of a new paper in *Science* settle on "sectarianism" as most reflective of the current political state, in which Democrats and Republicans dislike members of the other party more than they like members of their own.

"The existing words don't incorporate the moral component," says Northwestern University social psychology professor Eli Finkel, one of the paper's 15 authors. "They don't fully capture this idea that our views are morally right in this absolute sense."

The core of tribalism, for example, is kinship—members of a tribalistic group feel a familial bond with one another. The core of

"Political Sectarianism in America and 3 Things Driving the 'Ascendance of Political Hatred,'" by Clark Merrefield, The Journalist's Resource, October 29, 2020. https://journalistsresource.org/politics-and-government/political-sectarianism-political-hatred/. Licensed under CC BY-ND 4.0.

sectarianism, by contrast, is religion, faith and "moral correctness and superiority of one's sect," the authors explain.

In other words, a political sect isn't bonded in the way that a family is—a brother and sister might drive each other crazy but still innately love each other and remain bonded by blood. The authors argue that American political sects are bonded by faith that their side is morally superior to the other—echoing the ties that sometimes bind the religiously faithful. The effect is that politicians have little incentive to represent all their constituents in policy and lawmaking, since political sectarians rarely cross the aisle to vote for candidates outside their party.

There might be some logic to sectarianism if Democrats and Republicans disagreed not solely based on their party identification but on the underlying ideas their parties push. That's not the case, according to the authors, citing the 2015 paper "Red and Blue States of Mind: Partisan Hostility and Voting in the United States" in *Political Research Quarterly*.

The authors of the new paper, "Political Sectarianism in America," explain that "the causal connection between policy preferences and party loyalty has become warped, with partisans adjusting their policy preferences to align with their party identity."

It is not a purely academic exercise to develop accurate language to describe America's fractured politics. Rhetorical precision can help people understand real-life consequences, like the potential for violence on and after Election Day.

"The issue is when things get sectarianized, when the other side is so iniquitous—'those people are just so awful'—then the stakes seem high enough that violence in pursuit of your political aims becomes less unacceptable, that the violation of democratic principles becomes less unacceptable," Finkel says. "That makes sense because these are moral tradeoffs: 'I could compromise a little bit of democracy if it will increase the likelihood that the other side stays out of office.'"

It's Getting Cold in Here

Researchers at American National Election Studies, a collaboration between Stanford University and the University of Michigan, have for decades produced surveys during national election years that ask participants how "hot" or "cold" they feel about opposing parties. Researchers specifically ask about "feelings toward some of our political leaders and other people who are in the news these days."

Participants then rate their feelings toward politicians on a temperature-like scale, with 100 degrees being "very warm or favorable," 50 degrees indicating no feeling and 0 degrees being "very cold or unfavorable." The final result is what ANES calls "feeling thermometers." Political scientists commonly use ANES feeling thermometers in research on polarization.

Dubbing it the "ascendance of political hatred," the authors of the current paper use results from the past 40 years of ANES feeling thermometers to show that Democrats and Republicans "have grown more contemptuous of opposing partisans for decades, and at similar rates." Since 2012, "this aversion [has] exceeded their affection for copartisans."

Put another way, sectarian political divisions have become so entrenched over the past decade that Democrats and Republicans dislike members of the other party more than they like members of their own party. And yet "political sectarianism is neither inevitable nor irreversible," according to the authors.

Three Reasons—Three Solutions

The authors, an interdisciplinary group of political scientists, psychologists and sociologists, offer three reasons for the rise of American political sectarianism.

The first has to do with demographic sorting between the Democratic and Republican parties. The parties tend to cleanly sort between liberals and conservatives, as well as by educational, racial, religious and geographic categories. These "mega-identities," as the authors put it, can "change other identities, as when partisans alter their self-identified religion, class or sexual orientation to align with their political identity."

The authors note that this sorting by ideology and demographics has happened concurrent with Republicans and Democrats overestimating their aggregate differences.

"For example," they write, "Republicans estimate that 32% of Democrats are LGBT when in reality it is 6%; Democrats estimate that 38% of Republicans earn over $250,000 per year when in reality it is 2%," citing the 2018 paper "The Parties in Our Heads: Misperceptions About Party Composition and Their Consequences" in the *Journal of Politics*.

The second reason that the authors point to is partisanship in broadcast news media, particularly since Ronald Reagan's presidential administration ended the Federal Communications Commission's fairness doctrine in 1987.

Under the fairness doctrine, if radio and television broadcasters wanted to keep their FCC licenses, they had to offer a fair opportunity for contrasting viewpoints to be heard on issues of national importance, such as presidential campaigns. The doctrine wasn't without critics, but its termination presaged the rise of conservative pundits and news networks, like Rush Limbaugh and Fox News, and the leftward turn of networks like CNN and MSNBC. Today, social media echo chambers play an outsize role in perpetuating political sectarianism, according to the authors.

The final reason the authors offer for American sectarianism is that politicians and political elites themselves are more likely today to push ideologically extreme ideas and language, "with Republican politicians moving further to the right than Democratic politicians have moved to the left." Politicians in the major political parties have also become more financially reliant on donors who hold extreme ideas, the authors explain.

Yet there are pathways, both in terms of policy and personal accountability, to reduce political sectarianism, according to the authors.

The first pathway: Individuals who take it upon themselves to understand and correct misconceptions about members of the other party and to communicate directly with them. Such efforts may also include civil, religious and media leaders who are committed to "bridging divides," the authors write.

Social media interventions are another way to reduce sectarianism. Interventions might include crowdsourced judgments of news source quality being baked into algorithms so that hyper-partisan or false content doesn't often show up in users' news feeds.

The final pathway toward reduced sectarianism in America involves incentives for politicians to avoid polarizing language and policies. The authors suggest these incentives might include campaign finance reform and minimizing partisan gerrymandering to "generate more robust competition in the marketplace of political ideas" and elect fewer extremists to the federal government.

"In a very real sense, the government kind of does start with us," Finkel says. "If we have the inclination, we as in the general populace, to say, 'I am going to try to resist the most polarizing elements on my side or the other side and not retweet the most outraged people but rather the people trying to listen,' if we get a groundswell of that, I think there's a chance we could start to make a real dent in these problems."

CHAPTER 3

Does the Contemporary Media Environment in America Encourage Political Extremism?

Overview: What Do We Mean When We Talk About Media Bias?

Julie Mastrine

Julie Mastrine is a writer, artist, and director of marketing at AllSides. She frequently conducts research on media bias and created the AllSides Media Bias Chart.

M edia bias was on full display following an exchange during Dr. Rachel Levine's confirmation hearing last Thursday in front of the US Senate.

Dr. Levine is President Joe Biden's nominee for Assistant Secretary of Health and is transgender. During the hearing, Sen. Rand Paul (R-KY), who is also a physician, asked Dr. Levine about whether or not she believes minors are capable of making the decision to change their sex, by means such as hormone blockers.

Sen. Paul asked, "Do you believe that minors are capable of making such a life-changing decision as changing one's sex?" And later, "Do you support the government intervening to override the parent's consent to give a child puberty blockers, cross-sex hormones, and/or amputation surgery of breasts and genitalia?"

Both the left and right both covered the exchange quite differently, displaying numerous types of media bias. The left was more likely to add subjective qualifiers to characterize Sen. Paul's questions, to accuse him of lying, or to label him or his questions as transphobic; right-wing media was more likely to point out that Dr. Levine appeared to evade the question. Both sides used sensationalist language.

"Unpacking Media Bias in Coverage of Rand Paul, Rachel Levine Exchange," March 2, 2021, by Julie Mastrine, is © 2021 by AllSides.com. Used with permission.

Left-Wing Media Shows Subjective Qualifiers, Mudslinging, Sensationalism

Here's a smattering of left-wing headlines, plus one center, on the exchange. I've underlined keywords that indicate bias:

- Sen. Rand Paul <u>Slammed</u> for <u>Transphobic</u> <u>Questioning</u> During Dr. Rachel Levine's Confirmation Hearing on Capitol Hill [CBS Local]
- Rand Paul <u>Tried to Derail</u> Rachel Levine's Historic Confirmation Hearing with <u>Transphobic</u> <u>Misinformation</u> [Vox.com]
- Rand Paul Goes on <u>Unhinged Transphobic Rant</u> at Dr. Rachel Levine's Co … [LGBTQ Nation]
- Rachel Levine, 1st Transgender Nominee, <u>Deflects Inflammatory Questions</u> from GOP Sen. Rand Paul [6abc News]
- Rand Paul <u>Attacks</u> Rachel Levine over Supporting Gender-Affirming Care for Trans Youth [Metro Weekly]
- Sen. Rand Paul <u>Parrots Right-Wing Media Lies</u> About Trans Youth During … [Media Matters for America]
- Rachel Levine <u>Faces Transphobia</u> in Historic US Senate Confirmation Hearing [USA Today]

The outlets above demonstrate a few types of media bias. An easy one to spot is sensationalism. Sensationalism is when information is presented in a way that gives a shock or elicits an emotional response. Words like "slams," "lashed out," "scathing," and "showdown" usually indicate sensationalism. Here, we see the following keywords that indicate sensationalism: "**attacks**," "**parrots**," "**slammed**," and "**rant**."

Another type of media bias on display is mudslinging. Mudslinging is when the media attacks someone's character. Here, Media Matters (Left bias) accuses Sen. Paul of lying, Vox (Left) says he tried to "derail" the hearing, and *USA Today* (Center) accuses him of transphobia—accusations about his inner world, that he has poor character and harbors fear and ill will.

Finally, we see subjective modifiers presented as fact. Some of the subjective modifiers used in the headline samples above are "**unhinged**," "**inflammatory**" and "**transphobic**." All point to interpretations of Sen. Paul's underlying attitudes, beliefs and feelings that can't be objectively verified, but are the result of someone deriving meaning from his remarks.

Subjective modifiers are descriptors based on personal opinions, assumptions, beliefs, tastes, preferences, or interpretations; they reflect how the writer interprets something. They largely reflect the meaning derived from an event, so they are colored by the writer's specific perspective or lens and cannot be verified using concrete facts and figures. Someone else may come away with a different meaning of the same event.

There are objective modifiers—"blue"; "old"; "single-handedly"; "statistically"; "domestic"—for which the meaning can be verified through observation. On the other hand, there are subjective modifiers—"suspicious"; "dangerous"; "extreme"; "dismissively"— that are a matter of interpretation.

Subjective characterizations are okay in opinion and analysis reporting that is clearly labeled, but should be avoided in hard news pieces that are presented as fact. None of the above articles were labeled analysis or opinion.

Right-Wing Media Shows Sensationalism and Mudslinging

Right-wing media characterized the exchange much differently. They showed their bias via sensationalism, and by highlighting Dr. Paul's accusation that Levine dodged the question:

- Watch: Rand Paul <u>Hammers</u> Biden's Transgender Nominee on Child Surgery, Sterilization [Breitbart]
- "Very Complex": Dr. Rachel Levine <u>Dodges</u> Sen. Paul's … [The Daily Wire]

- "We Should Be Outraged": Rand Paul Presses Dr. Rachel … [The Daily Caller]
- Left Smears Sen. Rand Paul After Fiery Exchange with Biden HHS Pick [Fox News]
- HHS Nominee "Evades" Grilling from Sen. Paul on Trans … [Newsmax]
- Biden Health Nominee Pressed on Support for Genital Surgery for Children [The Epoch Times]

Some right-wing media outlets used toned-down descriptions of what Paul did, saying he "pressed" the nominee. This language is relatively neutral—to ask a question is to press for information. Yet others used sensationalist language, saying he "hammered" Levine or had a "fiery exchange" with her.

Others, such as Newsmax (Lean Right) and the Daily Wire (Right), focused on Paul's accusation that Levine was dodging the question. This may be considered to be slant, which is when journalists highlight, play up or focus on one particular angle.

Fox News (Lean Right) also engaged in mudslinging back at the left, stating that they had "smeared" Paul. However, that particular piece could be said to clearly be an analysis piece, as it was a headline from *The Ingraham Angle*, an opinion-based talk show. The others were not labeled analysis nor opinion.

Sensationalism Makes You Click

Both sides were sensationalist because sensationalism makes you click. When you see a headline that there was a "fiery exchange" or an "unhinged rant," it piques your curiosity. Editors use these tactics to make sure you click on their content so they can earn ad revenue. But as media consumers, we have to be aware that the way things are characterized are often used for this purpose primarily—to get us to click—at the expense of accurately describing what happened.

We also have to understand that media outlets serve partisan agendas. That's why they insult the other side or attempt to show them in a bad light with mudslinging. It's democracy 101: everyone wants to sway your opinion in their favor, and this is done via the news media. Your beliefs ultimately affect who you donate to, which politicians and news outlets you support, how you vote—even what you buy. Shaping your beliefs is big business, both politically and economically!

How to Report More Neutrally

It's perfectly normal to have different subjective characterizations of an event, which is often what makes journalism so biased. But it is possible for journalists to report in a neutral and unbiased way, giving you only the facts of what happened, and letting you make any subjective characterizations for yourself (or letting the opinion columnists handle it).

In my Google and DuckDuckGo searching, I found three non-inflammatory, relatively neutral headlines, from RealClearPolitics (Center), the *Epoch Times* (Lean Right) and Yahoo! News (Lean Left, but when you click the article, it's actually a reprint from Fox News—Lean Right).

The headlines were:

- *Rand Paul Presses Biden Nominee over Views on Giving Minors Hormone Therapy* (Yahoo/Fox)
- *Biden Health Nominee Pressed on Support for Genital Surgery for Children* (The Epoch Times)
- *Rand Paul vs. Rachel Levine: Do You Support Government Overriding Parental Consent on Puberty Blockers?* (RealClearPolitics)

All of these get to the crux of what happened without mudslinging, sensationalism and spin. What are some other neutral ways we could have constructed this headline? Perhaps:

- *Rand Paul Asks Levine Her Position on Child Transitioning*
- *Paul Asks Levine Her Position on Child Hormone Replacement, Genital Surgery*
- *Paul to Levine: Should government or parents make decisions on child gender treatment?*

- *Paul Asks Levine Whether Government Can Override Parental Consent on Trans Treatment*
- *Transgender Children: Paul Asks Levine Who Decides Their Treatment*

Are these headlines longer? Yes. Do they more accurately describe what happened? I'd also say yes.

Although journalists are incentivized to inflame things to get clicks, media consumers deserve just the facts. Unfortunately, we typically get spin, subjectivity and mudslinging instead. Reading media across the political spectrum and comparing headlines can be a bulwark against this, as well as learning how to spot the types of media bias.

Should We Deny Extremist Groups Access to Online Platforms?

Thomas Holt, Joshua D. Freilich, and Steven Chermak

Thomas Holt is the James Westfall Thompson Professor of American and African American History at the University of Chicago. Joshua D. Freilich is a professor in the Criminal Justice Department at John Jay College and codirector of the online databases US Extremist Crime Database (ECDB), the American School Shooting Study (TASSS), and the US Extremist Cyber Crime Database (ECCD). Steven Chermak is professor in the School of Criminal Justice at Michigan State University.

In the wake of an explosion in London on September 15, President Trump called for cutting off extremists' access to the internet.

Racists and terrorists, and many other extremists, have used the internet for decades and adapted as technology evolved, shifting from text-only discussion forums to elaborate and interactive websites, custom-built secure messaging systems and even entire social media platforms.

Our research has examined various online communities populated by radical and extremist groups. And two of us were on the team that created the US Extremist Crime Database, an open-source database helping scholars better understand the criminal behaviors of jihadi, far-right and far-left extremists. Analysis of that data demonstrates that having an online presence appears to help hate groups stay active over time. (One of the oldest far-right group forums, Stormfront, has been online in some form since the early 1990s.)

But recent efforts to deny these groups online platforms will not kick hate groups, nor hate speech, off the web. In fact, some

"Can Taking Down Websites Really Stop Terrorists and Hate Groups?" by Thomas Holt, Joshua D. Freilich, and Steven Chermak, The Conversation, September 15, 2017. https://theconversation.com/can-taking-down-websites-really-stop-terrorists-and-hate-groups-84023. Licensed under CC BY-ND 4.0 International.

scholars theorize that attempts to shut down hate speech online may cause a backlash, worsening the problem and making hate groups more attractive to marginalized and stigmatized people, groups and movements.

Fighting an Impossible Battle

Like regular individuals and corporations, extremist groups use social media and the internet. But there have been few concerted efforts to eliminate their presence from online spaces. For years, Cloudflare, a company that provides technical services and protection against online attacks, has been a key provider for far-right groups and jihadists, withstanding harsh criticism.

The company refused to act until a few days after the violence in Charlottesville. As outrage built around the events and groups involved, pressure mounted on companies providing internet services to the Daily Stormer, a major hate site whose members helped organize the demonstrations that turned fatal. As other service providers stopped working with the site, Cloudflare CEO Matthew Prince emailed his staff that he "woke up … in a bad mood and decided to kick them off the internet."

It may seem like a good first step to limit hate groups' online activity—thereby keeping potential supporters from learning about them and deciding to participate. And a company's decision may demonstrate to other customers its willingness to take hard stances against hate speech.

But that decision can cause problems: Prince criticized his own role, saying, "No one should have that power" to decide who should and shouldn't be able to be online. And he made clear that the move was not a signal of a new company policy.

Further, as a sheer practical matter, the distributed global nature of the internet means no group can be kept offline entirely. All manner of extremist groups have online operations—and despite efforts by mainstream sites like Facebook and Twitter, they are still able to recruit people to far-right groups and the jihadist movement. Even the Daily Stormer itself has managed to remain online after being booted from the mainstream internet, finding new life as a site on the dark web.

Drawing Attention

Efforts to knock extremists offline may also have counterproductive results, helping the targeted groups recruit and radicalize new members. The fact that their websites have been taken down can become a badge of honor for those who are blocked or removed. For instance, Twitter users affiliated with IS who were blocked or banned at one point are often able to reactivate their accounts and use their experience as a demonstration of their commitment.

When a particular site is under fire, people who hold similar beliefs may be drawn to support the group, finding themselves motivated by a perceived opportunity to express views that are opposed by socially powerful companies or organization. In fact, radicalization scholars have found that some extremist groups actively seek out harsh penalties from criminal justice agencies and governments, in an effort to exploit perceived overreactions for a public relations advantage that also aids their recruitment efforts.

Relations Between Tech Companies and Police

Internet companies' decisions about online expression also affect the difficult relationship between the technology industry and law enforcement. There are, for example, many examples of cooperation between web hosting providers and police investigating child pornography or other crimes. But policies and practices vary widely and can depend on the circumstances of the crime or the nature of the police request.

For example, Apple refused to help the FBI retrieve information from an iPhone used by a man who shot 14 people in San Bernardino, California, in 2015. The company said it wanted to avoid setting a precedent that could put its customers at risk of intrusive or unfair investigations in the future. And Apple has since substantially increased its protections for data stored on its devices.

All of this suggests the tech industry, law enforcement and policymakers must develop a more measured and coordinated approach to the removal of extremist and terrorist content online. Tech companies may intend to be creating a safer and more inclusive environment for users—but they may actually encourage radicalization and simultaneously create precedents for removing content in the face of public outcry, regardless of legal or moral obligations.

To date, these concerns have arisen suddenly and briefly only in the wake of specific events, like 9/11 or Charlottesville. And while opponents may shut down one or more hate sites, the site will likely pop back up elsewhere, maybe even stronger. The only way to really eliminate this kind of online content is to decrease the number of people who support it.

The US Media's Problems Are Much Bigger Than Fake News and Filter Bubbles

Bharat N. Anand

Bharat N. Anand is the vice provost for advances in learning at Harvard University and the Henry R. Byers Professor of Business Administration at Harvard Business School. His work focuses on digital strategy, media and entertainment, and organizational change.

The US media has come under intense scrutiny, with analysts, politicians, and even journalists themselves accusing it of bias and sensationalism—of having failed us—in its coverage of the presidential election. Critics across the political spectrum have said that fake news and cyberattacks played a big role in determining the course of events. The prevailing logic has an "if only" tenor: *If only* the media had been less swayed by shocking stories, *if only* bias in the media had been purged, and *if only* fake news had been eliminated and cyberattacks curtailed, the outcome would have been different. The presidential transition has been marked by the same attitude: *if only* the media were less distractible and headlines more accurate.

Thinking that way is tempting, but it misses the mark. The media did exactly what it was designed to do, given the incentives that govern it. It's not that the media sets out to be sensationalist; its business model leads it in that direction. Charges of bias don't make the bias real; it often lies in the eye of the beholder. Fake news and cyberattacks are triggers, not causes. The issues that confront us are structural.

To the question, *If the media were to cover the election again, with the benefit of hindsight, could we expect anything different?* my answer is a sobering no. This is for two reasons: the way news is

"The US Media's Problems Are Much Bigger Than Fake News and Filter Bubbles," by Bharat N. Anand, *Harvard Business Review*, January 5, 2017. Reprinted by permission.

produced and amplified (the supply side) and the way consumers process news (the demand side).

A caveat is in order. The analysis here is not concerned with which candidate deserved to win or whose message was "better." It is concerned with examining the media and its coverage, identifying its root causes, and understanding what we should expect going forward.

The Supply Side I: Connectedness Matters More Than Content or Money

Political campaigns are marketing campaigns, messages aimed at selling a product. Like marketers, politicians obsess over messaging (what journalists would call "content") and a few key metrics that historically have determined success: amount of television advertising, number of "foot soldiers," intensity of get-out-the-vote operations, and voter demographics. But in the last two contests in which Hillary Clinton has participated, the 2008 primary and the 2016 election, she won on most of these metrics—and lost the elections.

Two developments bear noting. First, and most obvious, traditional media is no longer the only way to spread the word. Any candidate can communicate directly and instantly with millions of people. Media companies are experiencing an extreme form of competition that comes with digital technologies: Everyone is a media company today.

Second, and even more significant, social media is distinct from traditional media in that it connects users to each other. This means that messages can spread far more easily and quickly (compare how often you share a TV ad and a tweet).

The implications are threefold:

The Best Product Doesn't Always Win

Even if you have the best product or candidate, if you run a hub-and-spokes campaign, you'll attract followers one by one. Create a product or candidate that connects users, and your message—and advantage—will spread rapidly. Apple learned this the hard way. For 20 years, starting in 1984, the Macintosh was superior to any PC. Yet by 2004 its market share was down to 3%. Apple had a great product, but Microsoft had a network of connected users. Because more people used PCs, and wrote software for them, they became the default choice for nearly everyone.

Many organizations and entrepreneurs miss this lesson. Focus only on creating the best content or product, and you can lose because of untapped user connections—a phenomenon I call the "content trap." It explains why firms that have anchored their strategies to content have ceded digital leadership to those that have focused on connections.

Consider the Scandinavian media firm Schibsted, which engineered an impressive digital transformation through a philosophy of connectedness. It focused its efforts on earning a majority share of Europe's digital classified advertising market (a product that connects buyers and sellers). It then shifted its news focus from great content to content rooted in the question "Can we help readers help each other?" During the volcanic ash crisis of 2010, what it offered wasn't prize-winning stories about the roots of the eruption or its health implications, but an app (Hitchhiker's Central) that allowed readers to share travel plans and offer rides to each other. Similarly, during the 2016 election, many American voters found journalistic content less relevant than what they were experiencing in their own lives.

Bigger Marketing Budgets May Not Pay Off

In a digital world full of product clutter, the best marketing campaigns spend nearly nothing. JC Penney spent no money on television advertising during the 2015 Super Bowl, yet its "mittens" campaign was one of the most watched. The campaign relied solely on Twitter and went viral by virtue of intentional spelling mistakes. Once a "connected" product draws in users, those users effectively become the sales force. Facebook, Uber, and Airbnb are all examples of this. Donald Trump spent only half of what Clinton did during the campaign.

Expectations Matter

In connected worlds, expectations about future growth affect what current users choose; people want to be on a winning platform. This has led to a strategy known as *vaporware*, a term for when firms announce strengths they may not possess or supposedly imminent product launches to draw users. Consider Trump's first words in the June 2015 announcement of his candidacy: "Wow. Whoa. That is some group of people. Thousands.... This is beyond anybody's expectations. There's been no crowd like this." This wasn't just a campaign message; it was an effort to shape expectations and trigger connectedness.

[…]

Competition Can Backfire

Competition and private firms operating in their self-interest typically lead to well-functioning markets. But that's not always what happens. A well-known exception occurs when externalities exist—side effects on other people or firms that aren't usually accounted for by private actors. (Canonical examples are cigarette smoking or pollution, or a store manager in a large retail chain pursuing actions that benefit his individual store but damage the parent company's brand.) In situations like these, following your self-interest (in this case, as a media firm) doesn't necessarily further the collective good, or even your own.

In 2009 Netflix needed high-quality content to grow its streaming business. It could get that content only from Hollywood studios. The studios had seen Netflix grow its DVD business for a decade, and now, with a stronger bargaining position in the streaming market—the first-sale doctrine that allowed any DVD owner to resell did not apply to streaming—they could have chosen not to license to Netflix and nipped it in the bud. But they granted licenses, and Netflix soon became the giant they hadn't wanted to see arise. Why did the studios act against their own interests?

If they could have collectively agreed not to license to Netflix, the result would have been different. But they couldn't. At first only Viacom relented, licensing archived *Beavis and Butt-Head* episodes. One show, it reasoned, could not a streaming giant make. But then everyone followed that logic.

It wasn't that the content providers didn't see what was happening; it was that they couldn't coordinate. It's why newspapers let Google crawl their content for Google News. It's why they handed content to Facebook for its Instant Articles format last year.

So, too, with the recent political campaign. If every media outlet had ignored Trump's rallies and rhetoric, it would have paid handsomely for one outlet to cover them. But once one *did* cover them, no others could afford not to.

These events coalesced dramatically toward the end of the campaign, when Trump announced a press conference in which he would ostensibly make a major announcement about President Obama's birth certificate (a lie that he had prolonged that had found traction in media coverage several years back). Nearly every media outlet showed up. How could they not cover a major announcement by a presidential candidate? But it was a sham— there was no real announcement, other than that there would be no more announcements on the subject.

This is the prisoner's dilemma of reporting amid competition: Following your self-interest does not always further the collective good. The situation generated one of the most dispiritingly candid statements ever from a media executive: Early in 2016, when the head of CBS was asked about the disproportionate attention given to Trump, he quipped, "It may not be good for America, but it's damn good for CBS."

The network wasn't alone. Cable news outlets enjoyed similar gains in 2016, marking it as their best year ever. Meanwhile, public trust in the press reached its lowest level in history.

The Demand Side: Consumers Consume What They Want To

One of the longest-standing debates in marketing is not *whether* advertising works, but *how* it does. One view is that marketing persuades consumers to purchase. Hear a song once, and you may not like it; hear it repeatedly, and you'll start to, regardless of how good or bad it is (hence the phrase "all publicity is good publicity"). Others argue that marketing merely increases awareness without altering beliefs. By this reasoning, repeated exposure to a song that doesn't match your taste might make you *less* likely to buy it.

Does media reporting change what we believe, or do our preferences shape what media we choose to watch in the first place?

Most research indicates that the latter is central: Our preexisting preferences largely determine what media we watch. One of the most reliable findings in the study of television entertainment is that viewers watch programs whose characters are like themselves. Older people watch shows featuring older characters, younger viewers watch shows featuring younger ones; the same goes for gender, ethnicity, and income. A similar effect is seen in news: We watch outlets whose reporting is consistent with our beliefs. Viewers who identify with the right are more likely to watch Fox, while left-leaning people are more likely to watch MSNBC. Similar differences apply to intra-network program choices, since programs on the same network can differ in their positioning.

These patterns in news-watching would be puzzling if all that news providers did was provide verifiably objective information. But like entertainment programs, news programs and channels differ in their positioning, in the way they report information (often referred to as *slant*), and in what information they report (*agenda setting*). News positioning matters—viewers watch news programs and channels whose positions match their tastes and beliefs.

This pattern of sorting on beliefs is amplified over time by various additional factors. The first is competition among media, which has increased as digital technologies have led to a vast number of new media outlets, each catering to more-niche tastes. The second is viewers' confirmation bias, which leads us to reject valid information that is not consistent with our beliefs. Confirmation bias is deeply rooted in human behavior. It affects not just how we process information but who we associate with, creating "filter bubbles." These bubbles are further reinforced by website algorithms designed to personalize the information we receive based on our past behaviors. Persuasive effects of the media also serve to solidify these bubbles. (And even small persuasive effects can have large effects in close elections.)

Each factor increases viewer polarization, which on certain measures has reached unprecedented levels. Together, they shape how we respond to bias in the media. Consider the debate over left and right media bias, which goes back several decades and has grown in intensity over time. Part of what makes discussions of bias so thorny is that we almost never agree on what bias is. Both the debate and studies tend to focus on what the media reports—on content. But studies show that content is not the only place where bias lives. In experiments, when two people with different beliefs view *exactly the same content*, their perceptions of bias differ.

Add it all up, and the implications are profound.

First, we watch what we believe, but what we *don't* watch, we *don't* believe. This is the effect of sorting based on beliefs.

Second, negative coverage can have unintended consequences. Hear a source you don't trust, and when it reports something inconsistent with your beliefs, you'll discount that thing even more. (The rare exception is when events are incontrovertibly verifiable—for example, the question of who said what on the *Access Hollywood* tape.) During the election season, more newspapers endorsed Clinton than any presidential candidate in US history. Papers with a tradition of endorsing Republicans endorsed her; papers with a tradition of not endorsing a candidate did, too. But none of it mattered; editorial content was essentially irrelevant.

Third, and for the same reason, charges of media bias can actually help an outlet. The more your favorite channel is alleged to be biased by people you disagree with, the more you'll watch it.

Trump wasn't the first to see this phenomenon: In Fox News's early days, senior executives often acknowledged that charges of bias appeared to help them. And it isn't specific to right-leaning voters. After the election, when Trump tweeted complaints about the *New York Times* and *Vanity Fair,* both outlets saw a rise in subscriptions. Charges of bias harden beliefs and reinforce polarization.

Particularly sobering is that all this has nothing do with the much-lamented problem of fake news. Get rid of all verifiably fake news, as Facebook and others certainly should, and filter bubbles, polarization, and charges of media bias will remain.

Where Does This Leave Us?

Three forces combine to create the media coverage of political campaigns we observe today: connected media, which spreads messages faster than traditional media; fixed costs and advertising-reliant business models in traditional media, which amplify sensational messages; and viewers' news consumption patterns, which leads to people sorting across media outlets based on their beliefs and makes messages they already agree with far more effective. Each reinforces the others. Without these enabling factors, even the best marketing campaign would go nowhere, and fake news or leaked information from cyberattacks would have little effect.

Fair questions have been raised about the lack of investigative journalism early in the campaign, false equivalencies in reporting, and the use of paid campaign operatives as experts on television news. But digital technology and business incentives exerted more influence over the media coverage than editorial decisions and missing voices did. The ratings bubble had as much impact as filter bubbles did. The forces at work here—the search for profitability, competition, and self-interest—are things we embrace as profoundly American.

Competition in the media leads to efficiency as well as to checks and balances—all good things. But it fails to internalize the externalities from profitable but sensational coverage. It leads to differentiation and more voices (also good, and what's been the focus of regulatory efforts) but also to fragmentation, polarization, and less-penetrable filter bubbles (dangerous).

It's tempting to stretch the analysis between marketing and politics too far. They are different in important respects. Most notable, in marketing you can win through strategies that exploit the big-event bias of media (through attention-grabbing rhetoric) and the beliefs of consumers (through allegations that discredit your competitors). These strategies draw in consumers who are right for your brand. But in presidential politics, the same approach is incredibly risky because when you win, you serve everyone, not just those who "purchased your product." Despite these differences, the same economics of information supply-and-demand that shape digital strategies in business are doing so in politics.

Which leads to my conclusion: Even if we could somehow push "reset," we would have to expect the same sort of coverage that we got. The problems are too deep and structural for anything else.

What's the way forward? There are no easy answers to the question. This analysis mainly points to solutions that *won't* work. Voluntary efforts at restraint by well-meaning journalists won't work, because of advertising-based business models and competition. Eliminating fake news won't change the fact that voters ignore ideas contrary to their beliefs. And it won't solve the media's structural challenges or change its incentives. Media companies, their regulators, and their customers—all of us—have to look for ways to confront these challenges. The stakes could not be higher.

Critics Are Exaggerating the Impact of Social Media on Political Polarization

Lee de-Wit, Sander van der Linden, and Cameron Brick

Lee de-Wit is a university lecturer in the Department of Psychology at the University of Cambridge. Sander van der Linden is professor of social psychology in society in the Department of Psychology at the University of Cambridge. Cameron Brick is assistant professor of social psychology at the University of Amsterdam.

Americans are more divided along party lines than ever before. In the past two decades, the percentage of Americans who consistently hold liberal or conservative beliefs—rather than a mix of the two, which is the case for most people—has jumped from 10 percent to over 20. At the same time, beliefs about the other side are becoming more negative. Since 1994, the number of Americans who see the opposing political party as a threat to "the nation's well-being" has doubled. This deepening polarization has predictable results: government shutdowns, violent protests, and scathing attacks on elected officials.

Why are we becoming more polarized?

There are probably many reasons. Could social media be driving polarization? Many people think so—and, indeed, Facebook, Reddit, and Twitter have all become sites of ferocious political argument. While polarization definitely plays out on social media, the evidence to date suggests that its impact is subtler than you might think. Social media, it seems, amp up moral and emotional messages while organizing people into digital communities based on tribal conflicts.

"Are Social Media Driving Political Polarization?" by Lee de-Wit, Sander van der Linden, and Cameron Brick, Berkeley, January 16, 2019. This article originally appeared in *Greater Good*, the online magazine of the Greater Good Science Center at UC Berkeley. For more information, please visit greatergood.berkeley.edu. Reprinted by permission.

This makes consensus building more difficult—but, as we'll discuss, it could also pave a more cooperative path forward.

Do We Live in "Filter Bubbles"?

Many people argue that we increasingly live in online filter bubbles that only expose us to the ideas we already agree with. This is consistent with a broader psychological literature on confirmation bias, showing that we are more likely to seek out and agree with views that align with our pre-existing beliefs. Selecting our preferred news sites and curating our social media accounts potentially makes it easier to listen to groups or individuals who validate our own worldviews.

The filter bubble idea has recently been elegantly demonstrated in the lab by Cass Sunstein and Tali Sharot and colleagues. The authors tested who participants would turn to for advice in categorizing geometric shapes—an obviously non-political task. In fact, this study found, participants preferred to seek advice from people who held similar political views, deciding that they must be more competent—despite evidence to the contrary!

If following people on social media who are more aligned with your worldview exacerbates polarization, then it follows that listening to "the other side" would reduce polarization. However, a recent experiment found essentially the opposite.

Christopher Bail and colleagues from Duke University recruited hundreds of Democrats and Republicans who were active on Twitter, and paid them to follow a Twitter bot that would retweet content from the opposing side. After a month of exposure, the Democrats retained about the same attitudes—but the Republicans ended up more conservative than when they started the study! This result suggests that polarization in the US could be driven by exposure to views people disagree with, rather than being separated from them by filter bubbles.

There are several ways of interpreting this result. For example, it could be that participants were reacting directly to the content of the messages they were exposed to on Twitter, but it could also be the case that they were simply responding to the messengers, not the message. In other words, the issues are not as important as group affiliation. Whatever the interpretation, this study suggests that more work is required to understand to what extent filter bubbles might drive political polarization.

A study by Levi Boxell and colleagues provided a simpler test of the role of the Internet: Is more social media use associated with more polarization? Boxell and colleagues assessed polarization in the US for different age ranges—and they surprisingly found that polarization was highest for the age groups that use the Internet and social media the least, such as older adults (75+).

This suggests that if the Internet is fueling polarization, its influence might be more indirect. This indirect influence is plausible, however, because in many traditional newsrooms, activity on social media has itself become news. Indeed, Trump has proved particularly successful in dominating the traditional news media (TV and print) with his activity on Twitter.

Thus, it is possible that the climate of debate on social media influences the tone of debate on other media platforms. Could social media influence polarization even in Americans who rely on the traditional media?

How Social Media Shape Debate

William Brady and colleagues tested what types of political messages on Twitter are more likely to be shared. When the researchers looked at tweets from the Presidential, Senate, and House of Representatives candidates in the 2016 US election, they found that tweets with more emotive and moral words were more likely to be retweeted. All voters responded more to words showing moral outrage, but effects were somewhat stronger for tweets from Republican candidates, and Republicans were more likely to respond to emotional words about patriotism or religion.

This work suggests that if politicians want to maximize their impact on Twitter, they need to resort to more moral and emotive vocabulary. This in turn might help explain why encouraging people to follow politicians from the opposing side appears to worsen polarization: Politicians tweet the policy positions that their political base wants to hear, of course—but they do so in moral and emotive language that may create negative reactions from the opposing side.

This language itself becomes news, as reporters turn tweets into headlines that can generate fear on the "other side." In this way, the whole news cycle shifts towards more polarizing and emotionally laden content.

According to Gordon Allport's "contact hypothesis," contact between groups lessens prejudice. However, decades of research testing this hypothesis has found some limitations. Although intergroup contact does tend to increase cooperation—and reduce prejudice—the positive effect may depend on important contextual factors, such as the nature of the conflict and whether the groups have equal status or a common goal. As Allport put it, sometimes more contact can lead to more trouble. That appears to be the case on Twitter.

Can We Build Social-Media Bridges?

So, perhaps we need to start thinking about how to structure interactions between groups on social media so that conflict becomes less likely and cooperation becomes more possible.

Social media companies need to do more themselves to counter online extremism and polarization by, for example, better regulating the political targeting of ads on their platforms. However, even in the absence of change in policy or on the sites themselves, there is a lot we can do as individuals to make social media less polarized.

A distinctive feature of social media is the importance of social consensus cues or online endorsement (e.g., likes, shares). Some research shows that the presence of these distinctive social cues can actually trigger decisions to select news in a way that reduces selective political exposure. In other words, if a story has been upvoted or shared a million times, it is likely to burst your bubble, even when the content is not ideologically congenial.

We can also try to cultivate a diverse network, extending beyond our immediate circles. It's not necessarily a good thing that social media increase the volume of information that we receive from people whom we already know well. Rather, research suggests that even when we are not exposed to the "other side" directly, so-called "weak ties" (friends of friends, acquaintances) offer a degree of political diversity that might inspire more political moderation.

Unfortunately, as the research we've discussed suggests, this diversity won't necessarily lead to harmony, since you're more likely to encounter strong emotional and moral language that could trigger negative partisan reactions. You might find the antidote in a trait known as Actively Open-Minded Thinking (AOT). AOT is a cognitive style that allows people to be more thoughtful, flexible, and open-minded, even when information contradicts a strongly held prior view. For example, both conservatives and liberals who score higher in AOT are less likely to display strong polarization on hot-button issues, such as climate change. Similarly, a new study earlier this year found that high-AOT Twitter users were better at creating and responding to social media content in a thoughtful and reflective manner.

In short, perhaps the solution to our problem is not completely out of reach. When we treat online spaces like we would treat our own community, difficult conversations become more productive. No matter how confident in our arguments or aggrieved we feel, everyone benefits when we actively try to be more thoughtful and open-minded about what we say—and how we react to others with whom we disagree—both online and offline.

Political Institutions Are More Responsible Than the Media Environment for the Rise of Extremism in American Politics

Michael Atkinson and Daniel Béland

Michael Atkinson is an attorney and the former inspector general of the Intelligence Community. Daniel Béland is the James McGill Professor of Political Science and director of the McGill Institute for the Study of Canada (MISC) at McGill University in Toronto.

In recent years, right-wing extremism has flourished in the United States. Last fall, for instance, the Tea Party movement encouraged the nomination of Republican midterm candidates like Sharron Angle, Rand Paul and Christine O'Donnell, whose views are well to the right of those of the median American voter. Although some of these candidates actually lost key midterm battles, the overall trend has been a radicalization of the right that makes bipartisanship hard to achieve. Earlier this year, in the House of Representatives, following the Tea Party's radical antigovernment agenda, Republicans such as Paul Ryan (Wisconsin) formulated controversial and arguably extreme proposals like the privatization of Medicare, one of the largest and most popular social programs in the United States. This summer, the debate over the federal debt ceiling saw the flourishing of radical proposals from Tea Party Republicans, including calls to dramatically reduce the size of government.

Although Fox News and other media outlets have played a major role in these developments, this extremist turn was in large part made possible by the design of American political institutions. Extremism may have its ultimate origins in the paranoid and conspiratorial dynamics of American political history, but it is American political institutions that enable the cyclical recurrence of

"American Democracy and Political Extremism," by Michael Atkinson and Daniel Béland, Institute for Research on Public Policy, October 1, 2011. Reprinted by permission.

extremism in American politics. It is not simply a matter of excessive partisanship produced by social forces and antagonistic world views. It is the amplification of these positions by an institutional architecture ill-suited to governing that has drawn increasing criticism from within the American political establishment.

Even before the Tea Party became such a central player in the political debate, close observers of the continuing American political drama had begun to despair about their political institutions. In an article describing the relative success of Germany in managing the recent recession, conservative columnist David Brooks described the United States as "an institutional weakling." On the left, in their 2005 book *Off Center*, Jacob Hacker and Paul Pierson called for institutional reforms aimed, among other things, at increasing political accountability. Far from lauding the genius of the American Constitution, there is a growing recognition that the United States faces a major institutional problem that the patriotic cult of the Constitution is increasingly unable to mask. This institutional problem, which makes current right-wing extremism so central in the first place, is America's extreme version of the separation of powers.

The separation-of-powers doctrine is praised by constitution makers around the world as the essential foundation of limited government, and Americans have taken a radical view of it. They have established a republic with a multitude of legislative forums in which credible arguments and interpretations of problems and solutions can be offered. A multiplicity of views is a good thing, but not when it immobilizes decision-making. In the 2009-10 debate over health insurance reform, a shower of legislative proposals and counterproposals contaminated one another, confused the public and provided unhelpful openings for demagogues and special interests. More recently, this summer, institutional uncertainty exacerbated the political drama over raising the federal debt ceiling, which was done just hours before the dead-line.

This unhappy spectacle of American democracy at work underscores the point that in an extreme separation-of-powers regime, there is no government and there is no opposition. The closest Americans come to a "government" is something called "the administration." The language is important. The Obama administration consists of all of those executive branch appointees, literally thousands of them, responsible for managing programs authorized and funded by Congress. As opposed to the situation prevailing in countries like Britain and Canada, for example, the president leads an appointed government, not an elected one.

It is true, of course, that political parties run the legislative affairs in both British-style parliamentary governments and the American Congress. We are used to contrasting these legislative bodies in terms of the degree of unity the parties demonstrate (that is, there is a higher level of party discipline in parliamentary systems than in the United States). But the difference is more profound than that. Consider what the parties in each legislature do once they have gained authority. In Congress, they elect their leadership; in parliamentary systems their leaders have already been elected. In Congress, the dominant party forms the majority, with one or two individuals, like former Republican senator Arlen Specter (Pennsylvania), shifting allegiances. In parliaments the dominant party or parties form the government. At the end of the process parliamentary countries have a government; the United States does not.

A similar condition applies with respect to the opposition. Because the elected president sweeps the field in a winner-take-all election, there is no constituted opposition left behind. In the case of a Democratic presidential victory like the one witnessed in November 2008, the Republican Party still exists, but its leader, the chair of the Republican National Committee, is not popularly elected and is seldom seen as a credible spokesperson. As happened after 2008 Obama's victory, thousands rush to fill the void and a handful of party leaders make a credible bid for the role, but the party that loses the presidential election has no formal constitutional responsibilities. In Congress, the senior members of the party do their best to muster a coherent message, but no one can prevent defeated vice-presidential candidates, upstart governors, self-proclaimed maverick senators or blustering talkshow hosts from claiming to speak for huge opinion blocs within the party.

This is exactly what happened after Barack Obama entered the White House in early 2009, as the Tea Party and politicians claiming to speak with a true conservative voice helped shape key political and policy debates. During the 2010 midterm primaries, Tea Party supporters successfully promoted the nomination of radical Republican congressional candidates like Rand Paul (Kentucky), who won a Senate seat at the midterm election. Although some Tea Party candidates like Sharron Angle (Nevada) and Christine O'Donnell (Delaware) lost, partly because of their extremist positions, it is undeniable that, during the two years following the election of Obama to the presidency, people like Sarah Palin filled the void on the right in the absence of a clear "opposition leader." Although the 2010 midterm elections, which led to a Republican majority in the House of Representatives, created a more institutionalized form of opposition, the true "opposition leader" will truly emerge only when the 2012 Republican presidential candidate is nominated. Meanwhile, Republican leaders in Congress, including Speaker John Boehner, must deal with the self-proclaimed, non-elected opposition of the Tea Party, which is likely to rebel if the duly constituted leadership fails to confirm extreme stances on a range of issues. The above-mentioned proposal to privatize Medicare featured in the broader but equally radical "Ryan Budget" illustrates the overt willingness of many House Republicans to make such stances on major issues in order to please their narrow electoral base, which is highly influential during the primaries. The behaviour of many Tea Party House Republicans during the 2011 debt ceiling debate provides more ground to this claim, as these actors complicated the negotiations between Democrat and Republican leaders by taking extreme stances on taxation and spending issues. For at least some House Republicans, taking such extreme conservative positions is probably the best way to secure their nomination in the 2012 Republican primaries, in which Tea Party supporters are likely to play key role.

The media are rightly being blamed for providing a platform for deliberately disruptive and meretricious commentary that has facilitated the emergence of the Tea Party. The late and unlamented program *Crossfire* looks embarrassingly civil when compared to the barbed broadsides that pass for journalism on Fox News. To make matters infinitely worse, the Internet has vastly increased the opportunities for falsehoods to flourish, with inspired rumours and innuendoes finding a field of voyeurs on YouTube. So the media is partly to blame for encouraging Tea Party-style extremism.

Yet the media merely amplify the polarization; it is American institutions that create the large windows of opportunity for political extremism. For instance, consider that the separation of powers makes every congressman a media target. With no authoritative voice to speak for the party and no singular government to take definitive positions, a strong element of fluidity is introduced into the policy-making process. Unlike Parliament, where a single bill is presented with the expectation that amendments will not alter its fundamental purpose, Congress sees a multitude of bills advanced with the expectation that they will be merged, gutted, abandoned or disavowed as the process unfolds. Members of Congress adjust their views in Washington based on how constituents and an organized groundswell like the Tea Party seem to be reacting to ever-changing policy proposals.

A fluid process sounds democratic. Good ideas can be tossed in from all directions, rapid adjustments made in response to public reaction, and opponents on one clause can be allies on another. But the very fact that individual lawmakers, and the administration for that matter, are free to change their minds creates a confusing "who's on first" scenario in which even close followers of the debate cannot be sure what is being considered by whom. It is in this confusion that lies and deceptions flourish. Because partisan mutual adjustment is valued in the system and practised by lawmakers on a continuing basis, claims regarding the true views of peripatetic policymakers cannot be lightly dismissed. In countries like Britain and Canada, Parliament does not operate this way. The much maligned tendency of party leaders to squelch public opposition on the part of caucus members has an upside. It is not difficult to determine a party position on any given topic, or determine that the party has no established view. And if the latter is the case, this is not an invitation for party members to float their individual trial balloons or express their personal convictions. It is an invitation to help establish in private a party position that all can defend in public.

In contrast, an extreme separation of powers privileges the mobilization of opinion blocs within civil society and allows diverse and often extreme positions a legitimacy they would be denied elsewhere. In the case of the United States, the process is vouchsafed by a commitment (more or less firm) to the acceptance of democratic outcomes and the protection of civil liberties. What this version of the separation of powers cannot deliver is accountability. Those who make accusations, including those who hold public office, and spread falsehoods are relatively immune from political disposal if they can protect a relatively narrow political base in their district and beyond. Allegations over "death panels" during the recent health care debate illustrate this sad yet institutionally embedded reality.

Within the British parliamentary system, MPs have no political base to shield them from the party's authority, with the result that citizens in parliamentary systems focus their attention on authorized political spokesmen for the dominant parties. A dramatic example of that is the political situation in Canada, where Conservative Prime Minister Stephen Harper has direct control over what his ministers and MPs say in public. In Canada, as in other parliamentary democracies, others who comment or offer advice are distinctly detached from a political process in which parties are the only ones in the bullring.

Many people believe that it is only the United States that has a separation-of-powers system, but that is incorrect. In Britain and Canada, for instance, the unity achieved by the concept of the supremacy of Parliament hides the multiple elements within Parliament that contest for power between elections. The difference is that the contest is regulated, the leadership is established and the locus of accountability is uncontested, at least in theory. None of this necessarily provides needed policy change, but there is a greater likelihood that when change comes, the opposition to it will be coherent and close to the views of the median voter. Extremism in opinion is a by-product of extremism in institutional design, as contemporary American policy and political debates attest.

This means that we cannot simply blame "American culture" or even the rise of the conservative movement for the contemporary politics of extremism in the United States. Although cultural and religious factors identified by people like Richard Hofstadter do play a role in the development of extremist opinion, it is American institutions that grant it legitimacy by deliberately fragmenting authority, and depriving the country of a coherent, institutionalized opposition. Although calls for moderation are always welcome, and potentially useful, institutional reform is the most effective way to reduce extremism in American politics. Americans do not need less partisanship, they need better partisanship. A way needs to be found to oblige parties to take greater ownership of their own agendas by insisting on adherence to party policy in exchange for the use of the party label. The dangers of conformism that such an innovation would invite pale beside the dangers of extremism that polarize the country and make good governance almost impossible.

The Increasing Power of Social Media Companies May Be at Odds with Democracy

Kalev Leetaru

Kalev Leetaru is a senior fellow at the George Washington University Center for Cyber & Homeland Security. His past roles include fellow in residence at Georgetown University's Edmund A. Walsh School of Foreign Service and member of the World Economic Forum's Global Agenda Council on the Future of Government.

Last week something extraordinary happened: Twitter briefly suspended the official account of the president of the United States, preventing him from posting until he deleted a tweet it said violated its rules. From merely hiding the president's tweets, as it had done before, the company briefly stopped him from tweeting altogether.

Then, three days later, Yelp announced it would start formally flagging businesses accused of racism based solely on media reports.

Those two developments crystallized once again a key question that increasingly shadows our age: How can the growing power of social media companies coexist with the foundations of democracy? A democratic society rests upon an informed citizenry free to openly debate their shared future. The First Amendment guarantees this, enshrining both the right of the press to cover the unvarnished reality of daily events and the right of the public to consider all ideas, even those possibly deemed harmful by the majority of society. Pundits who laud social-media censorship would do well to remember that calls for the rights we hold dear today, including universal suffrage and civil rights, were once deemed the same kind of "harmful" speech that in today's world would likely be banned by social media.

"Social Media's Role in Democracy: More Harmful Than Helpful?" by Kalev Leetaru, RealClearPolitics, October 14, 2020. Reprinted by permission.

Social platforms were once viewed as a way to promote democracy to the world, granting unfettered freedom of expression and unfiltered access to information. Today they enforce ever-changing opaque rules of "acceptable speech" and define "truth." Even more troubling, the journalism world is increasingly embracing Silicon Valley's new role as Ministry of Truth rather than condemning it.

Emboldened by the media's support for muzzling a president many news outlets despise, Silicon Valley companies have ramped up their censorship of elected officials. It was just five months ago that Twitter first visibly flagged an official statement of the US government as "misleading." With such censoring becoming almost routine now, it becomes front page news only when a social platform doesn't censor the president.

Yet Twitter's suspension of President Trump's Twitter account last week crossed a new line. What would have happened if a national emergency such as an earthquake or coordinated terrorist or cyberattack had struck during this period, with the president's ability to communicate with the American public compromised? Such disasters could have impaired Twitter's ability to quickly restore his access, and it is unclear if they would have done so even in a national disaster.

The courts have ruled that "Twitter is not just an official channel of communication for the president; it is his most important channel of communication." How is it, then, that a private company has the right to disable an official government communications channel from posting and Facebook has the right to delete an official government announcement? Unsurprisingly, neither company responded when this question was posed to them.

How do social media companies reconcile this censorship with the traditional norms of democratic societies? In 2018, a Facebook spokesperson offered only that "they're definitely important questions, but I don't have anything else to share right now." Asked again in light of their increasing action against the president, neither Twitter nor Facebook responded. Nor did either company respond when asked what would stop them from banning users or politicians calling for them to be broken up as monopolies.

Not content merely to rule the digital world, social platforms have increasingly stretched their reach over the physical domain. This past April, Facebook banned the use of its platform to organize protests that did not require social distancing. It subsequently quietly relaxed this ban for the George Floyd protests and has remained silent when asked whether it still enforces those rules regarding other such demonstrations.

Yelp continued this trend last week with its announcement that it would begin appending a "Business Accused of Racist Behavior Alert" warning label to reviews. Rather than rely on the due process of police reports, forensic media analysis and court rulings, the company's sole verification source will be news reporting. Given that media coverage itself can be misled by viral social campaigns, it is unclear how, precisely, the company will ensure its new effort is not manipulated. And given the #MeToo movement's split over the sexual assault allegation against Joe Biden, it is further unclear how Yelp will adjudicate the inevitable dual standards that will emerge and evolve.

Yelp's reliance on news reports for "verification" points to the larger problem confronting social platforms today: How to arbitrate truth? Take the example of conflicting guidance from public health authorities regarding spread of the coronavirus. Asked whether a post recommending masks would have been removed back in February for violating then-current CDC guidelines, a Facebook spokesperson acknowledged the difficulty of determining "truth" amidst the fast-changing scientific understanding of COVID-19 and suggested that government should step in rather than having private companies decide what to delete and what to permit.

Beyond their more overt actions of banning users, deleting posts, and setting "acceptable speech" rules, there lurks an even more powerful force impacting American democracy: the algorithms that increasingly customize what we see online.

The media once served as a bulwark against the narrowing of our national understanding of key issues. While the coastal elites of legacy news outlets were always given outsized influence on the news cycle and national conversation, local journalists would spotlight the events and concerns of their own communities, ensuring their voices could be heard in the national debate. But with the collapse of small-town journalism, the increasingly dominant coastal media often dismiss those concerns as the uneducated ramblings of "flyover country." Once-sacrosanct media ideals like "both sides" reporting are facing calls for elimination in order to stop promoting "nonsense" and "conspiracy" theories and Republicans' lies.

In their heyday, broadcast and print journalism exposed us to a cross-section of the day's events, broadening our horizons with the sometimes-serendipitous discovery of news and ideas we would not otherwise have encountered. In contrast, the algorithms that underlie our social platforms are designed to channel us towards content that provokes the emotional extremes most likely to engage us. Facebook's own internal research concluded in 2018 that "our algorithms exploit the human brain's attraction to divisiveness" and will feed users "more and more divisive content in an effort to gain user attention & increase time on the platform."

This can lead to almost parallel worlds of information awareness. In 2014, for example, Facebook users famously enjoyed lighthearted videos of friends and celebrities dumping buckets of ice over their heads for the ALS Ice Bucket Challenge, perhaps blissfully unaware there was anything amiss in America. Twitter users, meanwhile, saw endless livestreams of social turmoil as police and protesters clashed in Ferguson, Mo. Invisible algorithms steered their respective user communities towards two starkly different views of our nation.

As news is increasingly consumed through these digital platforms, the media landscape has begun to drift back toward the narrow parallel views of America that haunted the party-paper model. Viewers of CNN and MSNBC could be forgiven for believing that Portland, Ore., has been at peace the last four months and that Seattle's CHOP zone enjoyed a "summer of love." Fox viewers saw video of violent looters rampaging nightly in the streets, while the news channel's peers praised "peaceful demonstrations." Their only overlap was a fixation on imagery of law enforcement.

How can a democracy function when half the nation turns on the television, opens a newspaper or reads social media and sees an entirely different America than the other half? How can we reach consensus on issues ranging from policing to pandemic response when we're exposed to such different views of our nation?

In these partisan times, it can be all too easy to embrace Silicon Valley's censorship as a necessary evil to curb the flow of hateful speech and misinformation. The problem is that, by definition, a democracy represents the collective will of an informed people, not the arbitrary decisions of unaccountable corporations to determine what is allowed and disallowed.

To see where this path inevitably takes us, ask your helpful Amazon Alexa device, "Is Amazon a monopoly?"—and try running an ad campaign on Facebook questioning its answer.

Organizations to Contact

The editors have compiled the following list of organizations concerned with the issues debated in this book. The descriptions are derived from materials provided by the organizations. All have publications or information available for interested readers. This list was compiled on the date of publication of the present volume; the information provided here may change. Be aware that many organizations take several weeks or longer to respond to inquiries, so allow as much time as possible.

The Anti-Defamation League

605 Third Avenue
New York, NY 10158
(212) 885-7700
website: www.adl.org

Formerly known as the Anti-Defamation League of B'nai B'rith, the Anti-Defamation League (ADL) is an international Jewish organization based in the United States. The ADL's mission is to resist the defamation of the Jewish people and to promote justice around the world.

The Centrist Project

2420 17th Street, 3rd Floor
Denver, CO 80202
(703) 962-1354
email: campaign@centristproject.org
website: www.centristproject.org

The Centrist Project is a grassroots organization dedicated to organizing centrist Americans, supporting centrist policies, and encouraging more independent candidates to run for public office to put our country ahead of any political faction in order to solve problems.

Convergence Center for Policy Resolution

1133 19th Street NW
Suite 410
Washington, DC 20036
(202) 830-2310
email: info@convergencepolicy.org
website: www.convergencepolicy.org

Convergence Center for Policy Resolution is a 501c3 nonprofit organization focused on solving social challenges through collaboration. The Convergence team brings deep knowledge of policy and process and works with leaders and doers to move past divergent views to identify workable solutions to seemingly intractable issues.

Democratic National Committee

430 South Capitol Street SE
Washington, DC 20003
(202) 863-8000
website: www.democrats.org

Since 1848, the Democratic National Committee has been the home of the Democratic Party, the oldest continuing party in the United States.

FactCheck.org

Annenberg Public Policy Center
202 S. 36th Street
Philadelphia, PA 19104-3806
(215) 898-9400
email: editor@factcheck.org
website: www.factcheck.org

FactCheck.org is a nonpartisan, nonprofit "consumer advocate" for voters that aims to reduce the level of deception and confusion in US politics. It monitors the factual accuracy of what is said by major US political players in the form of TV ads, debates, speeches, interviews, and news releases.

FAIR (Fairness and Accuracy in Reporting)

124 W. 30th Street, Suite 201
New York, NY 10001
(212) 633-6700
email: fair@fair.org
website: www.fair.org

FAIR, the national media watch group, has been offering well-documented criticism of media bias and censorship since 1986.

Independent Voter Project

PO Box 34431
San Diego, CA 92163
(619) 207-4618
email: contact@independentvoterproject.org
website: www.independentvoterproject.org

The Independent Voter Project (IVP) is a nonprofit, non-partisan 501(c)4 organization dedicated to better informing voters about important public policy issues and to encouraging nonpartisan voters to participate in the electoral process.

Pew Research Center

1615 L Street NW, Suite 800
Washington, DC 20003
(202) 419-4300
website: www.pewresearch.org

Pew Research Center is a nonpartisan fact tank that informs the public about the issues, attitudes, and trends shaping the world. It conducts public opinion polling, demographic research, media content analysis, and other empirical social science research. Pew Research Center does not take policy positions.

PolitiFact

1100 Connecticut Avenue NW
Suite 440
Washington, DC 20036
(202) 463-0571
website: www.politifact.com

PolitiFact is a fact-checking website that rates the accuracy of claims by elected officials and others who speak up in American politics.

Reason Magazine and Reason.com

1747 Connecticut Avenue NW
Washington, DC 20009
(202) 986-0916
website: www.reason.com

Reason is the monthly print magazine of "free minds and free markets." It covers politics, culture, and ideas through a provocative mix of news, analysis, commentary, and reviews. *Reason* provides an alternative to right-wing and left-wing opinion magazines by making a principled case for liberty and individual choice in all areas of human activity.

Republican National Committee

310 First Street SE
Washington, DC 20003
(202) 863-8500
website: www.gop.com

The Republican National Committee is a US political committee that provides national leadership for the Republican Party of the United States.

Southern Poverty Law Center
400 Washington Avenue
Montgomery, AL 36104
(334) 956-8200
website: www.splcenter.org

Southern Poverty Law Center monitors hate groups and other extremists throughout the US and exposes their activities to law enforcement agencies, the media, and the public.

Bibliography

Books

Barry J. Balleck. *Modern American Extremism and Domestic Terrorism: An Encyclopedia of Extremists and Extremist Groups.* Santa Barbara, CA: ABC-CLIO Books, 2018.

J. M. Berger. *Extremism.* Cambridge, MA: Massachusetts Institute of Technology Press, 2018.

David Cox. *The Most Dangerous Course of Action: The Next Decade in Transnational Terror and Domestic Extremism.* North Charleston, SC: CreateSpace Independent Publishing Platform, 2013.

Jeff Flake. *Conscience of a Conservative: A Rejection of Destructive Politics and a Return to Principle.* New York, NY: Random House, 2017.

Jonathan Haidt. *The Righteous Mind: Why Good People Are Divided by Politics and Religion.* New York, NY: Vintage Books, 2012.

John Kasich. *Two Paths: America Divided or United.* New York, NY: Thomas Dunne Books, 2017.

Matthew Levendusky. *How Partisan Media Polarize America.* Chicago, IL: University of Chicago Press, 2013.

Mike Lofgren. *The Party Is Over: How Republicans Went Crazy, Democrats Became Useless, and the Middle Class Got Shafted.* New York, NY: Penguin Books, 2012.

Thomas E. Mann and Norman J. Ornstein. *It's Even Worse Than It Looks: How the American Constitutional System Collided with the New Politics of Extremism.* Philadelphia, PA: Basic Books, 2012.

Jon Meacham. *The Soul of America: The Battle for Our Better Angels*. New York, NY: Random House, 2019.

Josh Neal. *American Extremist: The Psychology of Political Extremism*. Perth, Australia: Imperium Press, 2020.

David Neiwert. *Alt-America: The Rise of the Radical Right in the Age of Trump*. New York, NY: Verso, 2017.

Greg Orman. *A Declaration of Independents: How We Can Break the Two-Party Stranglehold and Restore the American Dream*. Austin, TX: Greenleaf Book Group Press, 2016.

Christian Picciolini. *Breaking Hate: Confronting the New Culture of Extremism*. New York, NY: Hachette Books, 2020.

Gabriel Sherman. *The Loudest Voice in the Room: How the Brilliant, Bombastic Roger Ailes Built FOX News—and Divided a Country*. New York, NY: Random House, 2014.

David Michael Slater. *Wingnuts: A Field Guide to Everyday Extremism in America*. Mechanicsburg, PA: Sunbury Press, 2021.

Charles J. Sykes. *How the Right Lost Its Mind*. New York, NY: St. Martin's Press, 2017.

Charles Wheelan. *The Centrist Manifesto*. New York, NY: W.W. Norton & Company, Inc, 2013.

Periodicals and Internet Sources

Russell Berman, "What's the Answer to Political Polarization in the US?" *Atlantic*, March 8, 2016. https://www.theatlantic.com/politics/archive/2016/03/whats-the-answer-to-political-polarization/470163/

Nate Cohn, "Polarization Is Dividing American Society, Not Just Politics," *New York Times*, June 12, 2014. https://www.nytimes.com/2014/06/12/upshot/polarization-is-dividing-american-society-not-just-politics.html

Brett Edkins, "Report: US Media Among Most Polarized in the World," *Forbes*, June 27, 2017. https://www.forbes.com/sites /brettedkins/2017/06/27/u-s-media-among-most-polarized -in-the-world-study-finds/#6c810c122546

David French, "On Extremism, Left and White," *National Review*, May 30, 2017. http://www.nationalreview.com /article/448108/political-extremism-beleaguers-both-left -and-right

Joshua Hersh, "Extremism Experts Are Starting to Worry About the Left," Vice News, June 15, 2017. https://news.vice .com/en_ca/article/3kpeb9/extremism-experts-are-starting -to-worry-about-the-left

Zolan Kanno-Youngs, "White House Unveils Strategy to Combat Domestic Extremism," *New York Times*, June 15, 2021. https://www.nytimes.com/2021/06/15/us/politics /biden-domestic-terrorism-extremists.html

Michael Kazin, "A Kind Word for Ted Cruz: America Was Built on Extremism." New Republic. October 29, 2013. *https://newrepublic.com/article/115399/history-american-extremism-how-unpopular-opinions-became-mainstrea*

Cynthia Miller-Idriss, "Extremism Has Spread into the Mainstream," *Atlantic*, June 2021. https://www.theatlantic .com/ideas/archive/2021/06/us-fighting-extremism-all -wrong/619203/

Robert O'Harrow Jr., Andrew Ba Tran, and Derek Hawkins, "The Rise of Domestic Extremism in America," *Washington Post*, April 12, 2021. https://www.washingtonpost.com /investigations/interactive/2021/domestic-terrorism-data/

Shaun Raviv, "Divided We Fall: Georgia State Researchers on the Factors Driving Polarization and Extremism in America," *Georgia State University Research Magazine*, January 2021. https://news.gsu.edu/research-magazine /divided-we-fall

Jennifer Rubin, "Opinion: Here's What Is Missing from Biden's New Domestic Terrorism Strategy," *Washington Post*, June 15, 2021. https://www.washingtonpost.com /opinions/2021/06/15/heres-what-is-missing-bidens-new -domestic-terrorism-strategy/

Niall Stanage, "The Memo: Homegrown Extremism Won't Be Easily Tamed," *The Hill*, June 15, 2021. https://thehill.com /homenews/the-memo/558622-the-memo-homegrown -extremism-wont-be-easily-tamed

Matthew Valasik and Shannon Reid, "After the Insurrection, America's Far-Right Groups Get More Extreme," The Conversation, March 15, 2021. https://theconversation.com /after-the-insurrection-americas-far-right-groups-get -more-extreme-156463

Index